BETWEEN THE NIGHT AND ITS MUSIC

WESLEYAN POETRY

Edited and with an Introduction by Lauri Scheyer

A. B. SPELLMAN

BETWEEN THE NIGHT

AND ITS MUSIC

New and Selected Poems

Wesleyan University Press Middletown, Connecticut

Wesleyan University Press
Middletown CT 06459
www.wesleyan.edu/wespress

Manufactured in the United States of America
Designed and composed in Arno Pro by Mindy Basinger Hill

Library of Congress Cataloging-in-Publication Data
available at https://catalog.loc.gov/
cloth   ISBN 978-0-8195-0119-6
e-book   ISBN 978-0-8195-0120-2

5   4   3   2   1

CONTENTS

This book opens, as it should, with A. B. Spellman himself announcing his arrival into the world and explaining his childhood background:

When Rosa Belle Bailey Spellman was due to deliver her first child, she moved into her mother's house in the hamlet of Nixonton, on the out-skirts of Elizabeth City, North Carolina. They had a good midwife there. And so, Alfred Bennett Spellman, Jr. was born probably on August 7th, 1935, but officially on August 12th. Family lore has it that the midwife suffered a mental breakdown the next day and failed to get the papers to the courthouse. Such birth day confusion is not unusual to people who were born in the South during that time. From the beginning, Rosa would call the child A. B. and the father Alfred so that there would be no confusion about who should answer.

Two dominant factors describe Spellman's early years: the Great Depression and Jim Crow. His parents were frugal strivers who devoutly believed that education was the route to social standing and economic security. They were the first in their families to finish high school. Alfred, Sr. was an untrained painter and as such was considered a community asset. People would bring their children to sit for portraits in a time when very few Black households owned cameras. Rosa, an avid reader, was the brains of the family; it was she to whom the teachers would turn when they needed a formal letter or a paper drafted. They, as teachers (Rosa would complete her degree when A. B. was in high school), knew better than anyone that the Jim Crow education that was available to their son was insufficient for his needs, and they created a community scandal by sending A. B. to a new Catholic elementary school in the 6th grade. The boy was a tireless reader who grew his mind in an environ-ment where the sole bookstore sold few books of any literary value and there was no Black library, etc.

Otherwise, his only youthful exposure to arts and culture came from radio broadcasts of the Jazzbo Collins Show that he could sometimes pick up from New York, and weekly broadcasts of the Metropolitan Opera carried by a station in Norfolk, Virginia.

Spellman attended Howard University as a political science major and earned his BA degree in 1956. Amiri Baraka (before 1965, known as LeRoi Jones) and Lucille Clifton were among his classmates and his professors included Owen Dodson (Drama), John Hope Franklin (History), and Arthur P. Davis and Sterling A. Brown (English). Never having traveled to "the big city," Spellman arrived at Howard wearing an outfit he had spent the whole summer selecting: a wide-collar, powder-blue houndstooth jacket and pegged pants in the style of a zoot suit, only to encounter students whose fashion image was closer to Brooks Brothers. He soon met and became friends with Baraka/Jones, who was recollected by Spellman:

He knew a great deal about jazz and used to rave about a high school tenor saxophonist who was his friend, Wayne Shorter. Though he was the leader of our group, at that time LeRoi did not exhibit the greatness that we celebrate him for today. I started seeing signs of an elevated mind in his correspondence from his time in the military. While in the Air Force, his letters became more serious than I had ever known him to be. He read hard books and had hard comments and questions about them. *Finnegan's Wake*, for example, which I have never been able to get through. He had thoughts and questions about the state of the world that I had never heard from anyone, student or faculty. He was thinking and searching.

Spellman thought "Surely New Jersey must be the coolest place on earth" if it produced people like Baraka/Jones. As a student at Howard, Spellman was mainly reading works of philosophy and took few courses in literature: "I was reading Kierkegaard and Sartre and existentialists and was just dying to try it out on people." Spellman credits Dodson as his main influence as a professor. In his second year of college, Spellman joined the Howard Players and was cast in the starring role of "He" in *He Who Gets Slapped* (the play that was the basis for the 1924 silent film, which contributed to the stardom of Norma Shearer and Lon Chaney). After long philosophical arguments about how to interpret and present the title line ("I am he who gets slapped"), director Dodson threatened to replace Spellman with a Drama major, and the young actor quickly agreed to deliver the line as instructed. Spellman's only creative writing class was taught by

Dodson, who gave him the advice to "write what you know," and Spellman has followed that dictum throughout his literary career.

Spellman took one drama class with Sterling Brown, and the biggest regret of his college education is that he didn't take full advantage of the opportunity to benefit from Brown's knowledge, erudition, and charm, which he came to appreciate with further contact after he had graduated. He especially recalls the extraordinary stories Brown would tell, both folktales and entirely imaginary yarns that Brown called "lies." Spellman particularly recalls one long visit to Brown's house where he felt he truly got to know him for the first time. As Spellman puts it: "Damn, I'm sorry that I didn't make notes on that afternoon at his house (now two blocks from where I live). I recall only fragments of a whopper that he told that ended with, 'and that's when that German woman shot Du Bois in the ass with a .22 pistol.'"

According to Spellman, "I was very interested in Sterling Brown's interest in and use of the African American vernacular. I was impressed by the way that he adapted the toast, what are often called 'jailhouse poems' in the hood, Shine, Stack O' Lee, The Signifying Monkey, etc., as models for some of his pieces, 'The Ballad of Joe Meek,' for example. He probably was the reason that I wrote 'The Joel Blues.'"

"The Joel Blues" first appeared in issue 8 (1961) of *The Floating Bear*, was reprinted in Spellman's 1965 collection *The Beautiful Days*, and is included in this book. Written for Joel Oppenheimer, this poem opens "I know your door baby / better than I know my own . . . It's been so long since I seen you / I feel like you done up & gone." Explicitly a blues poem, here we can see how Brown's emphasis on African American folk materials, especially the musical traditions originating in spirituals and related forms, encouraged Spellman to incorporate Black popular music and references in his poetics. This pattern has extended throughout Spellman's nearly 70-year career both as a poet and as a music critic. Thinking back to Brown's influence, Spellman muses "on 70-year-old memories from an 87-year-old man." As Spellman recollects, "I believe that more of us looked to Brown than to any other of our antecedents in poetry as a model. When those of us who had begun our career (if poets can be said to have 'careers') with an art for art's sake orientation and had to find a Black voice and attitude, Brown was essential."

While Spellman stresses his regret at not taking better advantage of

Brown when he was a student, he was able to absorb and decide to use Brown's example in his later life more fully. Says Spellman, "I was very impressed that Sterling Brown remembered me as a student twenty years later, even though I was very trifling in his class. That he was so caring, so accessible, so down-to-earth was a model for the kind of person I wanted to be. Also, that he had such a love for Black people as they are, and not as some intellectual like Du Bois wanted them to be, was inspirational, e.g., Du Bois thought that jazz was socially destructive."

After graduating from Howard, Spellman thought of the examples of poets like William Carlos Williams, Archibald MacLeish, and Wallace Stevens, who had professional as well as literary careers, and decided he should go to law school, though he had no particular interest or aptitude. Ranked third in his class, he nonetheless was dropped from law school for "lack of seriousness of purpose." During that time of finding his path, Spellman moved in for a few months with Baraka/Jones who first got him into jazz writing. As Spellman says, "I'm still living off things he taught me then."

Spellman moved to New York City in the summer of 1957 and became actively involved in the arts scene of Lower Manhattan. He describes himself at the time as "largely an acolyte" of Baraka/Jones, but then became more independent as he gained confidence and experience:

> I grew out of that status sometime in the mid-'60s. I followed him into jazz writing and, though I had been writing poetry since my sophomore year at Howard, I had to seriously raise my game to hang out with the people who attended his Friday night salons at his apartment in Chelsea. We're talking Ginsberg, Creeley, Olson, Corso, Wieners, Oppenheimer, di Prima, Selby, Duncan, etc. & whoever else was in town. I had a lot of catching up to do. Can you imagine an argument between Creeley and Corso on structure?

Other highlights of this period of his life included his "near-nightly presence at the Five Spot during Thelonious Monk's return to jazz performance and the blooming of John Coltrane in the Monk quartet." In 1959, Spellman started working as a writer, reviewing music for magazines including *Metronome* and *Downbeat*. During the New York years, he conducted a daily wakeup program on WBAI on topics ranging from jazz to literature, for instance the poetry of Paul Blackburn. His interview with Malcolm X, taped in Harlem, was later broadcast on WBAI (March 19, 1964), and subsequently published in the periodicals *Monthly Review* and *Revolution* (https://monthlyreview.org/2005/02/01/interview-with-malcolm-x/). Spellman left WBAI when the station manager was fired for remarks he made about Vietnam, which were critical of America's bombing of civilian facilities.

During those extremely productive years, Spellman firmly established his reputation for "persistent relevancy" as a "poet, historian, and critic," as described by journalist Nat Hentoff. In 1965, Diane di Prima's Poets Press published Spellman's first book of poems, *The Beautiful Days*, with an introduction by Frank O'Hara, which opens with "Spellman writes lean, strong, sexy poems," and closes with "He's honest, so naturally a lot of them are perfect." Long out of print (though more recently made available as a limited-edition facsimile), *The Beautiful Days* has been treasured by readers and poets for generations. Poems from that slim volume are often anthologized and are well represented in *Between the Night and Its Music*. Spellman earned added acclaim during that period with his still classic book, *Four Lives in the Bebop Business* (originally published by Pantheon, 1966), a detailed study of jazz musicians Cecil Taylor, Ornette Coleman, Herbie Nichols, and Jackie McLean, which has been many times reprinted by several presses (currently available as *Four Jazz Lives* from the University of Michigan Press). The relationships among poetry and the other arts, notably music and painting, are longstanding and central themes of his critical and creative writing.

In 1967, the same year that Baraka left Lower Manhattan and moved to Harlem, Spellman moved to Atlanta. He met and married Karen Edmonds, the subject of numerous poems in *Between the Night and Its Music*, who was actively involved in the Student Nonviolent Coordinating Committee (SNCC) as director of research. During this period in Atlanta, Spellman served as poet-in-residence at the Atlanta University Center and Emory University, as well as doing television commentary, which included film, music, and theatre reviews. In the late 1960s, it became apparent to Spellman, Edmonds, and others that Atlanta lacked arts centers in the Black community although the foundation of a strong cultural life existed. Local universities actively hosted events there and several professional actors such as Samuel L. Jackson emerged from the theatre programs at Spelman and Morehouse. Spellman recalls that there were some good local jazz musicians and figures like Bernice Johnson Reagon who came out of the Civil Rights movement. At that time in Atlanta, Reagon—who later became known as the founder of Sweet Honey in the Rock—was running the Harambe Singers and the Freedom Singers, which Spellman describes as "the vocal arm of SNCC." It was a time and place of burgeoning creativity involving other activists such as Ethiopian artist Alexander "Skunder" Boghossian, who had been in Paris in the late years of the Negritude Movement and later became an influential faculty member and mentor to young Ethiopian artists at Howard University. A new poem in this volume entitled "Skunder" serves as an elegy to this important and memorable figure.

To try to coalesce the existing energy and talents, Spellman and Edmonds together founded the Atlanta Center for Black Art in 1968. Spellman argues that it is always a mistake to try to precisely date the start of any movement because the seeds have been sown long before, as is true of the Black Arts Movement. As he recounts:

> John O'Neal started Free Southern Theatre several years before Baraka moved to Harlem, Samella Lewis had visual arts going on the West Coast, Elma Lewis started a center in Boston, the great Katherine Dunham founded a museum and cultural center in East St. Louis nearly fifteen years earlier, and there were still organizations around that were founded during the WPA years. Then there were vestiges of the Harlem Renaissance that still survived. Nonetheless, Baraka was very important as a stimulus for the Black Arts Movement. He was tireless in going from city to city and showing people how they should go about setting up organizations. This was an example of giving up a career as that generation's success story since they seem to allow one per generation. Nevertheless, it was a kind of abandonment of that career in favor of establishing a cultural institutional presence in the Black community, and that was an inspiration to Black artists all around the country.

Baraka's example was reflected in the formation of the Atlanta Center for Black Art and Spellman's subsequent decision to go to work for the National Endowment for the Arts (NEA), where he could help transform support for arts and culture at a national level.

In 1969, Spellman became a visiting lecturer at Douglas College followed by a teaching stint at Livingston College (both in New Brunswick, New Jersey), before moving to Harvard University (1972–1975), where he taught African American studies, jazz biography, and African American cultural history, and ran the poetry workshop. His main piece of advice to his poetry workshop students was, "Go for it. You can do anything in poetry that you can pull off." During those years he also was a commentator on the *Say Brother* show on WGBH television.

Spellman moved to Washington, DC, in 1975 to begin his career at the National Endowment for the Arts (NEA). In his first years as program director he was called on to run Expansion Arts, which, according to Spellman, was "pretty much vilified by the arts establishment because they thought it was more social work than art and I was the person responsible for defending it." The goal of Expansion Arts was to fund arts organizations in inner cities and rural and tribal communities. Spellman held this position at the NEA for approximately fifteen years before moving on to other roles. He is especially proud of his earliest years in advocating for what was then an extremely controversial concept: Art should be provided for people who had little access to the arts in their communities.

According to Spellman, "You use everything you have" in making artistic decisions, and accordingly, he applied his taste and judgment as an editor, poet, and critic in his new role at the NEA. Rather than a pause in his literary career, the NEA years were an extended period of directly applying his knowledge and experience to transform the public art climate and expand opportunities in America. Spellman believes he was effective in promoting the democratization of national arts funding and appreciation, precisely because he was foremost a poet: "Understanding how to build something on a blank page helps you understand how to build an organization." It was a fortuitous moment for Expansion Arts to flourish in DC and the national environment. As Spellman reflects, "There was the Black Arts Movement, the Hispanic Arts Movement, the Native American Arts Movement, and there were exciting things happening there. This art was made in a very different way from how art is made within mainstream institutions." Spellman recollects:

Back in the 1970s, I developed a line of reasoning, because it made sense to me, about 21st-century American art. I thought there would be two factors that would very much affect 21st-century American art: one was new technology, which we could already see coming in the '70s, and two was the participation of people who would operate outside of the classic European tradition. That was obvious to me because I could see it at the ground level. To me, the cultural quality of any city is what happens with ground-level artists: new artists, young artists, and artists who work and provide culture in areas that had been largely deprived of cultural institutions even though they were culture rich. In a plural society, there will be a pluralism of standards, with jazz as an example. It has always been part of the mythology of Western art that there is one standard, and it is the standard of the court, not the standard of the community, and that bias is something we had to fight against. We're talking about a time when Gian Carlo Menotti said there would never be jazz at the Spoleto Festival because jazz was commercial music, and this was the prevailing attitude of the large culture-presenting institutions.

In painting this scene, Spellman was determined to promote standards of taste for paintings, poetry, and other arts that did not fit "the usual forms" familiar to American audiences. It was a battle and yet an extremely exciting opportunity to diversify ideas about arts producers and audiences. He remained at the NEA for thirty years and retired as deputy chairman in 2005. On his retirement, Spellman's service to and impact on the NEA was recognized by the establishment of the A. B. Spellman Award for Jazz Advocacy.

Because of federal conflict-of-interest rules, Spellman was prevented while working for the NEA from publishing in the nonprofit press or giving readings in nonprofit venues, including colleges and universities, "which basically means you can't publish or give readings." Because he chose to use the NEA opportunity to serve the literary and cultural community nationally, his prominent early presence as a poet, critic, and editor who was actively publishing his own and others' writings and giving readings was put on hold during this thirty-year period, though he continued to write sporadically, especially in his last five years at the NEA. There were frequent requests to reprint his poems during his time at the NEA, and his reputation remained strong, but because new work did not appear, his image has sometimes been that of an important figure only in the 1960s–1970s.

Between the Night and Its Music is intended to resolutely change such impressions. While Spellman's significance for the Black Arts Movement is undeniable, and the early work more than stands the test of time, his newest poems are among the most important and artful of his career.

Since leaving the NEA, Spellman has been a frequent commentator on National Public Radio (NPR), including being co-presenter of the NPR Basic Jazz Record Library series with Murray Horwitz. He has lectured frequently at various colleges and universities, conferences, and festivals. On an ongoing basis, he conducts public interviews with jazz masters at the New Mexico Jazz Festival. Since retiring, Spellman has mainly devoted himself to "getting his chops back" in writing poetry, which he has achieved *con brio.*

Spellman explains his decision to resume writing: "About twenty-five years into my time at the Endowment, it occurred to me that if I were to die, my children would have to put on my tombstone, 'Here lies Dad, he wrote great guidelines.' And I'm thinking 'No, no, I can't have that; I've got to recover my identity as a poet and set about writing poetry again.'"

He assigned himself many of the same exercises that he had given years earlier to his own poetry students, including writing what he described as very bad sonnets for his daughter and doing translations, a method recommended by Ezra Pound. He went to museums and started to write poems to paintings. As Spellman discovered, "The muscles weren't working. I always felt I'd go back to poetry but didn't anticipate how difficult it would be." But ultimately, he found it was "like riding a bike": the poetry muscles eventually came back stronger than ever, as evidenced by the extraordinary new poetry in this book, which extends and augments his powerful earlier oeuvre.

Three years after his retirement, his second poetry book, *Things I Must Have Known* (Coffee House Press, 2008), a full-length collection, was published to great acclaim and with a national reading tour. This book earned an Honorable Mention from the Gustavus Myers Outstanding Book Award and a nomination for the NAACP Image Award in Literary Work in Poetry. In April 2008, Spellman served as the poet-in-residence for National Poetry Month at California State University, Los Angeles (Cal State LA), which was made possible by an NEA Audience Development grant intended to increase access to the arts in communities—a program whose origins lay in Spellman's own work in the Expansion Arts program. Spellman's work at the NEA and as a practicing poet had formed a continuous totality. A highlight of the Cal State LA residency was a reading of love poems (written both by Spellman and middle school poets) in a packed auditorium of four hundred students at Chester W. Nimitz Middle School in Huntington Park, a school whose minority enrollment is 99 percent.

Spellman, historically regarded as one of the founding figures of the Black Arts Movement, is essential to include in any survey of American poetry from the 1960s to the present. His early poetry was published in the most prominent avant-garde journals of literature and culture of the era, and similarly to Baraka—with whom he had publishing as well as personal ties—he served as a bridge between groups of then-underground literary and artistic movements and artists, including the Beats, Black Arts Movement, New York School, San Francisco Renaissance, and Black Mountain communities. Spellman and Diane di Prima were the original editors of the renowned magazine *The Floating Bear*, and Spellman's first book was published by di Prima's Poets Press. Spellman served as a contributing editor of *Kulchur* and published his work in historically significant journals that are now receiving major scholarly and reader attention, including *Yugen* and *Journal of Black Poetry*.

A small number of signature poems have since become canonical, appearing in virtually every major anthology of African American poetry of the past fifty years, including *Understanding the New Black Poetry* (ed. Stephen Henderson), *Dices or Black Bones* (ed. Adam David Miller), *Poems Now!* (ed. Hettie Jones), *Black Fire* (ed. Amiri Baraka and Larry Neal), *Beyond the Blues* (ed. Rosey Pool), *Trouble the Water* (ed. Jerry W. Ward Jr.), and *The Poetry of Black America* (ed. Arnold Adoff). Spellman's continuing importance and centrality are proven by his inclusion in recent anthologies, such as *The Norton Anthology of African American Literature* (ed. Henry Louis Gates, Jr. and Valerie A. Smith), *Angles of Ascent: A Norton Anthology of Contemporary African American Poetry* (ed. Charles Henry Rowell), *Every Goodbye Ain't Gone* (ed. Aldon Lynn Nielsen and Lauri Ramey), *African American Poetry: 250 Years of Struggle & Song* (ed. Kevin Young), and *In Search of Color Everywhere* (ed. E. Ethelbert Miller).

Between the Night and Its Music: New and Selected Poems provides a rich representation of poems from Spellman's entire career from 1958 through

2024. Readers and critics have long been calling out for such a volume, since so much of Spellman's poetry has been inaccessible and inadequately documented, which has prevented a full and accurate showing of the scope and trajectory of his career. This book fills an urgent need for several reasons. Spellman's poetry is highly regarded, yet a small percentage of his work is in print. Only his 2008 collection *Things I Must Have Known* and individual poems in the most recent anthologies are available, with *The Beautiful Days* out of print. Ironically, some of the poems for which he is most acclaimed, such as "Did John's Music Kill Him?," are uncollected and appear only in anthologies. His voluminous body of poetry written since 2008 appears in print for the first time in this book. His reputation largely rests on his very early poetry from the 1960s, but some of his most powerful verse has been written in the past fifteen years.

For a prolific poet, Spellman has published a relatively small percentage of his writing and remains renowned on that basis alone. His reputation surely will be further enhanced with the publication of this expanded representation of his poetry and the insights provided in this volume. When viewed comprehensively, his nearly sixty years of poetic production place his achievements in a dramatically illuminated light, compared to the experience of reading individual and mainly early poems in the more specific context of the Black Arts Movement and Civil Rights eras. Although his indelible place in that historical moment is fully and accurately represented in these pages, this new book reveals Spellman's very current appeal.

As a volume of new and selected poems, *Between the Night and Its Music* includes brand new poems that have never been published, along with a selection of poems from across Spellman's entire career, including selections from *The Beautiful Days* and *Things I Must Have Known*, as well as poems that were previously uncollected, appeared only in magazines, or are long out of print. In other words, this book is a representative record of A. B. Spellman's poems from the 1950s to 2023. This full-length collection is an important milestone for several reasons. Very few poets have been able to sustain a career of such duration, and even fewer poets have continued to grow and evolve over time. He has created a body of poetry that has spoken in a strong and distinctive voice from his youth. The earliest poems stand up remarkably well and many of them feel as fresh and relevant as they did when they were first written. Even so, his most recent poems are among his most brilliant. They reveal the polish and mastery he has gained over half a century of reverence, love, and dedication to his medium. While racial themes and issues of civil rights and justice are indisputably at the core of Spellman's personal and literary ethos, he has achieved that goal to which Paul Laurence Dunbar and others have aspired: to be regarded and respected as a poet whose race is a factor in his identity but whose writing encompasses an expansive range of human and cultural issues with stylistic dexterity and variety.

It would be remiss not to note Spellman's lasting impact as a jazz critic. Along with Baraka's *Blues People*, Spellman's *Four Lives* and his other writings about jazz remain foundational texts among music lovers. In examining his music criticism and poetry, we see that Spellman's writing is not so neatly segmented. He considers himself foremost as a poet—though obviously a brilliant writer on jazz—and it is impossible to imagine Spellman's poetry without the presence of music and musicality. He has a keen awareness of sound, rhythm, mellifluousness, dissonance, of the cross-cutting and interweaving of sonic and semantic themes. In the poems, there are numerous repeated words and phrases, onomatopoeia, alliteration, rhythmic shifts juxtaposed with rapid shifts in narrative direction, themes that travel, transmute, and return. Many of his poems are dedicated to or inspired by musicians from many styles and genres, including Jellyroll Morton, John Coltrane, J. S. Bach, Bob Marley, Gonzalo Rubalcaba, and Franz Schubert. His poems are also infused with sensitive awareness of the other arts, from sculpture to dance, and we see many poems dedicated to or inspired by artists—again from many different periods, nationalities, and styles—among them Skunder (Alexander Boghossian), Van Gogh, and Jackson Pollock. Spellman is a deliberate and thoughtful crafter of imagery. Our senses and minds are continuously being taken to places we never expected.

These are some of the technical reasons why many of Spellman's strongest poems sound like more than language, more than purely literary or textual creations. They also feel like an ensemble of sensory instruments. Yet these are also deeply thinking poems. A reader may be reminded of Metaphysical poets such as John Donne, who developed his ideas and understanding of the meaning of life by working through (and enacting on the page) the process of writing his poems. As with Shakespeare's propositional sonnets, or the wit of Alexander Pope, or Emily Dickinson's pithy lyrical arguments, or the ingenious double voicing of Paul Laurence Dunbar, Spellman's poems are not merely imagistic or sensory, though they are that too—these are poems that engage with ideas as much as the senses.

This book is a tribute to a writer who is not exclusively a jazz poet or a Black Arts poet or even an American poet, but a poetic artist in English whose work will stand the test of time. In the fifteen years since his second book was published, Spellman has continued writing with renewed urgency and dedication.

*

Spellman's career might be viewed in three segments, to date: the early work gathered in *The Beautiful Days*, the middle period of *Things I Must Have Known*, written forty years later, and now the full flowering of one of our most gifted living poets in this momentous book.

What makes an A. B. Spellman poem? From the time of early poems like "John Coltrane An Impartial Review" to his magnificent new Van Gogh suite, the poems aren't self-referentially about the poet or the act of poetry writing: They are generously focused on the subject of the poem, which is why they take us to far-flung realms of the imaginative and experiential worlds. Spellman poems are never unilinear. They contain multiple interwoven themes, which often include juxtapositions of diction that take enormous mastery to handle—otherwise the writing would sound like a jumble of conflicting registers and directions. In "Ink Spots," we begin with an autobiographical reminiscence in lines 1–2 ("when I was a boy / the Ink Spots were a crossover quartet") leading us to assume we are embarking on a sentimental journey to revisit the poet's early musical memories. Even before the opening stanza ends, the adult voice intrudes to call out the dark underside of racial burlesquing, minstrelsy, and exploitation ("you may think of this as jim crow jovial / so securely hard core it was a chuckle all around"). The poem juggles roman and italicized stanzas that alternate between the Ink Spots' honeyed crooning and the "nightmare land" of systemic racism represented in baseball, servant classes, and Brown v. Board of Education, as the speaker grows to be "ashamed / of the Ink Spots and all the accommodating / black stars." We travel a complex road as Spellman dexterously navigates what otherwise might be seen as a confusing narrative. Unwilling to compromise by pretending this is a purely innocent lyrical tale, Spellman insists on the path of appropriate ambiguity and complexity. The poem's surprise ending finds the speaker trying and failing to convince his granddaughters that the Ink Spots' "high precise phrases / were good singing." The poem forces us to face the truth that social context cannot be ignored even when experiencing pleasure in Black cultural products, creating a challenging and rich sociohistorical texture characteristic of Spellman's poetry.

Stylistically, his poetry is audacious: the same words repeat in different grammatical categories and with startling accruals of fresh meaning often engineered with deft line breaks. At the start of a Spellman poem, we think we're on solid ground, but by the end, we're shaken and even a little disoriented to see where the poet has craftily taken us and where we have wound up ("After Vallejo" is one of numerous examples). I typically read Spellman poems in a circular way: at the end, you really need to go back to the beginning, multiple times, to figure out what the journey was. One almost needs to map it out to see the sheer delight and ingeniousness of how stanzas logically follow previous stanzas, and yet those Spellman twists and turns take us constantly by surprise.

In his work, Spellman repeatedly demonstrates that no topic worth contemplating is simple. There are always multiple avenues of entrance and exit and detours within. Contemplation leads us to another characteristic feature of Spellman's poems: They are lyric poems about ideas, people, art, life, pain, loss, love—all those big abstractions that are basically what we care about most. These poems are baroque, metaphysical, and completely of the current moment. It's a treasure to have such a major body of writing from any author. Spellman reveals poetry's ability to serve as a cultural and historical record and an aesthetic object of lasting beauty that transcends boundaries of time and space.

Here is an essential voice whose legacy continues building at a steady pace now that poetry is once again the center of his attention in addition to his devoted roles as father, husband, and grandfather. With new poems from 2008 to the present, some of his freshest and most skillful to date, Spellman continues to "bop to the bass line," as he puts it in "Groovin' Low."

Honored to serve as editor of this book, I wish to express my deepest gratitude and respect to the poet. It has been one of the most meaningful experiences of my life and career to be granted the opportunity to closely observe the example of A. B. Spellman, who displays with constant grace the brave challenges of revealing life's tensions, conflicts, and joys in beautiful literary form.

Note: All unattributed quotations are taken from interviews and correspondence between A. B. Spellman and Lauri Scheyer.

JOHN COLTRANE: AN IMPARTIAL REVIEW

may he have new life like the fall
fallen tree, wet moist rotten enough
to see shoots stalks branches & green
leaves (& may the roots) grow into his side.

around the back of the mind, in its closet
is a string, i think, a coil around things.
listen to *summertime*, think of spring, negroes
cats in the closet, anything that makes a rock

of your eye. imagine you steal. you are frightened
you want help. you are sorry you are born with ears.

NOCTURNE FOR ERIC

my eyes are better than
good but the night is far
away & i can't see the rain
that falls in my face.

street sounds, the wet clothes
clamped to my skin, come to no more
easy focus. everyone walks
at a great distance.

you are as clear to me as
anything, yet i see you thru
in, a window, framed. i could
hang you on a wall, if i was closer

FOR WHITE

my friend who drinks is a large man
in a small house at the end of a tube
where no english is heard
at the far end whatever day
gestures in spanish towards
the tube. is never seen from the house
what do you paint from a hole in a day?
paint eyes / burn the shadows /get down
what wildness the drink showed you
cover your favored demon
with the blood tones of fire
paint the day moving away

AFTER READING TU FU

the world is flat again &
beautiful women jaded but not with jade
& my hopeless poor who live for death
& children & a superior music fashioned
from blues
make as many mountains on the mind's horizon
as those nicely murdered politicians
handsome in profile / murderous in deed
coequal in death with my lovely city poor

if tu fu could find a poverty in silk
& poems in the wretched tribesmen he passed
in pushing his emperor's lust to "new frontiers"
then i will draw my lines in black around
yes, the commuters' army in glen plaid uniforms
whose borders run from wall street to westchester
whose disease is the fever of things
that's tu fu's meat

only one man ever dies in tu fu's ugly plain
he wills our wishes to the clouds
who hang them on the mountain
where his poems make water of us all

THE TWIST

a dancer's world
is walls, movement
confined: music

god's last breath.
rhythm: the last beating
of his heart. a dancer

follows that sound, blind
to its source, toward walls
with others. she cannot dance alone

she thinks of thought
as windows, as ice around the dance
can you break it? move

'64 LIKE A MIRROR IN A DARKROOM,
'63 LIKE A MIRROR IN A HOUSE AFIRE

A New Year's Day Poem

the newly dead silly
my best sentiments by an absence
more vital than memory. how
write for them except say the difference
in potency between a. b. & the newly
dead is barely measurable.

a. b. & the newly dead. we could sing together.
a quartet of my own familiar, with a. b. singing
bass. we'd sing for people like us.

this is what i feel for the newly dead:
they are like knots in a cord from me
to the first one. liebling, my tenor
loved boxing & ate himself to death. tristan
tzara, my baritone, left poems like insane orphans
to bother me in my home. john w. drank as much as i do.

that's '63 backwards: a passage of names
into graves: one man i knew by his mind's seminal
flutter; another by the way he kept himself alive.
i want to care about each longer than it takes
to write & correct these lines.

if i can care for the newly dead as far as from here /
to here /
i may be thought not to be among them.

THE BEAUTIFUL DAY V

he went
to the window
it folded & shrank

quietly & without warning
them, night leaked
into the room, into the 'idea'
of the group

how easy it is to lie
to you. what a soft
lie your silence is

she moved
to the window
night
shifted & sank

THE BEAUTIFUL DAY VI

came down from the sky &
settled
          on my eye   this
is what snow
                does   there
you go   an object
                    of snow
the day
          melts into water

BALTIMORE ORIOLE

CONSIDER OUR EYES, THOSE BRIGHT GLOBES that stand out in
our faces like some unlikely stones, burning, in a soft soil.

the lines in our faces
talk for us: that i'd knit
the lights of our eyes to make
a proper fabric to roll you in.

in firelight expose
the raw flesh under,
as a day the eyes provide.

will night in any light come
bright to us? anything living
be visible, held in our fingers
& tasted on our tongues?

& vernacular become a loveless habit?

JELLY WROTE

jelly wrote,
> you should be walking on four legs
> but now you're walking on two.
> you know you come directly from the animal famulee

& you do. but dr jive
the winding boy, whose hands' only work
was music & pushing
'certain ignorant light skin women' to the corner
was never animal

was never beast in storeyville, refining
a touch for ivory on pool green
with the finest of whorehouse ragtime; use even
for the 'darker niggers music. rough,' jelly wrote
'but they loved it in the tenderloin.'

o the tall & chancy, the ladies'
fancy, the finest boy for miles around,
'your salty dog,' but with diamond incisors,
shooting the agate under a stetson sky
his st louis flats winked into

aaah, mr jelly

THE JOEL BLUES

> after & for Joel Oppenheimer

i know your door baby
better than i know my own
i know your door baby
better than i know my own
    it's been so long since i seen you
    I feel like you done up & gone

in the morning in the evening
in the daytime & the nighttime too
in the morning in the evening
in the daytime & the nighttime too
    it don't matter what i'm doing
    all i got to think about is you

well the sun froze to the river
& the wind was freezing to the ground
o the sun froze to the river
& the wind was freezing to the ground
    if you hadn't heard me calling
    i don't think i ever could been found

o i ain't no deacon baby
i ain't never been a praying man
i ain't no deacon baby
i ain't never been a praying man
    i had to call to someone
you the only one was close to hand

i'm a easy ridin' papa
i'm your ever lovin' so & so
i'm a easy ridin' papa
i'm your ever lovin' so & so
 don't think i don't hear you callin'
 'cause i'm coming when you want to go

it's a pity pretty mama
that i go to look for you at all
it's a pity pretty mama
that i go to look for you at all
 but if it wasn't for the looking
 i'd be climbing up & down the wall

2008

DEAR JOHN COLTRANE

dead night has me writing poetry
in another hotel room. j. s. bach
is on the radio. the *keyboard concerto
in f minor*: the one you also hear
on oboe or violin. the largo
second movement begins
& the book in my hand drops
the room fades
& i put my reason down
to trail the bach of endless line
along this earthless path, each note full
& bright, a brilliant footprint on the dark
thru beauty, past knowledge, into
that state that shines too much
to be wisdom, is too transparent
to be art. i catch a fear of the place
where he will lower me when
this transporting melody closes
then it closes on itself & here i am
dear john, back at the beginning, better

later, different station, cold room dimming
it's you, john, *trane's slow blues*
now it's your line that opens, & opens
& opens, & i'm flying that way again
same sky, different moon, this midnight
globe that toned those now lost blue rooms
where things like jazz float the mind
this motion the still & airless propulsion
i know as inner flight. this view
the one i cannot see with my eyes
open. i hear the beginning approach, &
i know the line i traveled was a horizon
the circle of the world. another freedom
flight to another starting place

if i believed in heaven i would ask
if you, j. c., & bach ever swap infinite fours
& jam the sound that light makes
going & coming, & if you exchange maps
to those exclusive clouds you travel thru
& do you give them names?

GROOVIN' LOW

my swing is more mellow
these days: not the hardbop drive
i used to roll but more of a cool
fox trot. my eyes still close
when the rhythm locks; i've learned
to boogie with my feet on the floor
i'm still movin, still groovin
still fallin in love

i bop to the bass line now. the trap set
paradiddles ratamacues & flams
that used to spin me in place still set me
off, but i bop to the bass line now
i enter the tune from the bottom up
& let trumpet & sax wheel above me

so don't look for me in the treble
don't look for me in the fly
staccato splatter of the hot young horn
no, you'll find me in the nuance
hanging out in inflection & slur
i'm the one executing the half-bent
dip in the slow slowdrag
with the smug little smile
& the really cool shades

AFTER VALLEJO

i will die in havana in a hurricane
it will be morning, i'll be facing southwest
away from the gulf, away from the storm
away from home, looking to the virid hills
of matanzas where the orisha rise, lifted
by congueros in masks of iron, bongoseros
in masks of water, timbaleros in masks of fire
by all the clave that binds the rhythms of this world

i'll be writing when i go, revising another
hopeful survey of my life. i will die of nothing
that i did but of all that i did not do
i promised myself a better self
than i could make & i will not forgive

you will be there, complaining
that i never saved you, that i left you
where you live, stranded
in your own green dream

when you come for me come singing
no dirge, but scat my eulogy in bebop
code. sing that i died among gods
but lived with no god & did not suffer
for it. find one true poem that i made
& sing it to my shade as it fades
into the wind. sing it presto, in 4/4 time
in the universal ghetto key of b flat

i will die in havana in rhythm. tumbao
montuno, guaguanco, dense strata
of rhythm pulsing me away
                            & the mother of waters
will say to the saint of crossroads
well, damn. he danced his way out after all

THINGS THAT I MISS FROM MY YOUTH

1. Shooting Stars

night
made a luminous
& speckled hood
over my southern town
the milky way
was solid white
gods of all lands
could ride across it

you stitched together
your own
constellations
& they were the gods
who rode

every night thin
white streaks etched
the velvet black
you & your friend
watched for them
but they seemed
to fall in
only one eye
           decorating
those perfect hours
before sleep

now i must travel
great distances to find
a textured sky. now

light broadcasts up
from the city
                    now night
depopulates
the heavens

now
only the great
round moon
bears fantasy

2. *A Hometown I Could Walk Across*

it took
about an hour
at a pace that
allowed the notice
of birds & victory
gardens &
                    how do's? to
the old folks swinging
on their porches

i knew them all
by face, most
by name

they called me
after my father
little alfred

the houses all looked
right according to what
i knew: the fine ones
by the river
where the gentry
lived, the shotgun
flats where most black
folks lived
the two-box frame
ones in between

even the empty ragged
houses that sagged
into ruin
& melded
with the weeds
looked right
i knew time &
the fat brown
earth
would consume them

i did fear
the tall grass
where rattlers
& copperheads
might live

i now walk
in the city &
i still fear
the high grass

3. Hummingbirds

before she died
my mother complained
the little yellow
bird she liked
so much
never came by
her window
any more

she tried
to remember its song
& hated
to think it
might be gone
its color
went so well with
the hot green outfit
my hometown sported

i miss hummingbirds
more. they
have no song
no color no
shape & a funny
long beak

i remember their
movement & think
of modern dancers'
astonishing darts
to unexpected
places, startling
as shooting stars

hummingbirds love
to hang still
in space
with their beaks
in bright flowers

give them a song
& what kid
wouldn't want
to be a hummingbird

4. Aunt Julia's Mushy Fried Mullet

she stuffed her
house with the paper
flowers she made
screaming things
so loud

you thought you
smelled them—too
sweet for nature
but it was her
perfume you smelled
it weighed a ton

her custom bought
every flower

*

mother
said sis julia
was a fast young
thing. i do know
she married
six men &
divorced none. this
caused her much stress
when social security
got computers

true: aunt julia died
went to heaven &
returned with news of
the celestial chorus
& which kin
soloed in it, etc
the bastards laughed
at her

aunt julia
couldn't cook
a lick, but i loved supper
with her. why
didn't hummingbirds
hang 'round her? she
had the color
of her flowers &
the sweetness
of her perfume

too rich to find
in the world

5. Pay Envelopes

little sacks
of cash they put
in your hand
at 6 o'clock on
saturday

insufficient
by miles
but tangible
not metaphysical
like today's invisible
wages with
less body
than aunt julia's
holy ghost
whose mass she
almost could
calibrate

i miss
silver dollars &
fifty cent
pieces. big
rocks of money
you tied up
in a kerchief or
a sock
the sock knot
could make
a weapon

in a schoolyard
fight with the bully
big 6
oodiboy used
it so: a sort of
money bludgeon

i guess oodiboy's
doing well now

THINGS THAT I DON'T MISS FROM MY YOUTH

1. My School Books

often the covers
were loose
the inside front
was a directory
of the white school
across town

debbiejean &
skipper hall & tippie
tommy & terry
tebbetts. their
scribbles in
the margins
their doodles by
the headings

they had fingered
all the learning
before the books came
to us. our knowledge
was handmedown

used, discarded

it wasn't just
that the signs
regulated
what you ingested
where you voided

white fountains colored
fountains; white
toilets
colored toilets

& it wasn't just that
their nice word
for us was colored
making us into
something someone
had taken
a crayon to
it was
that they defined
our limits down
to our viscera
downtown
was theirs & we
could not carry
our effluents
to it
        my only passage
from this verdant wasteland
was books & other vagrant
art: opera from the met
on saturdays. bebop
from jazzbo's purple
grotto on clear nights
                its sound starlight thin
from the stretching
of its wavelength

i walked
most often to
the one bookstore
six blocks from relief

& after a poor snack of
the caldwells, maughams &
spillanes
out to the rat's
shelter in the alley
to solve
my bladder's urgent
imagination

3. *Not Knowing Better*

florene barco moved
to philadelphia &
on a visit home told
us she went
to school with
white kids
it was a lunar image

everything shouted
inferior
to us
        the patterns
we walked. the ease
with which they
commanded. that
we could not live

by the river
word of lynching
farther south & of course
the signs. i
thought it all to be
as much of nature
as the night sky
the birds of the air

the notion of place
meant not where
you stood but how
you talked
to a white man

place was
the wet brown earth
your knees
sank down in

& philadelphia
was the crescent
moon

4. Aunt Bud's '30 Something Chevy

ugly little black coupe
she wouldn't get rid
of tho aunt bud
was the only one
in the family
with money

unctuous woman, she
drove it thru homes
taking something of the life
she found there
she thought some
poor, blacker
than her, families
bad & carted
their kids to church
at 10c a head when
gas cost a nickel

she collected clothes
for poor folks
in the country, gave
them out at hog
killing time &
brought home hocks
& hams, offering
us the chitterlings
but we hated chitterlings
they stank
the house for days

aunt bud took
in kids from her baddest
families & worked
them toward salvation
for 5c an hour
              she taught
waste not
& made them eat
their ice cubes

a few years
with aunt bud &
the boys became
winos & the girls
whores & that chevy
took her to
more lives to empty

we'd call it
a classic today

WHY DO THEY CALL IT A NIGHTMARE
WHEN A HORSE IS WHAT YOU NEED?

i hate it, this dream
where the thing of indeterminate mass
gimlet eyes drilling at the back of my head
breath that bears the heat
of hell is after me & i'm running hard
trying to put a few skyscrapers between me
& it on my way out of town
i'm thinking: i've got plenty of time
this prowling theriomorph is slow
tho it's ugly as pain
but my goddamn feet take me nowhere
& the street that looks solid enough
becomes this treadmill that rolls under me
& shit! the big fuzzy lump is gaining

you've probably dreamt this too. your beast
closing, your laboring legs failing. maybe
you've looked it up, even consulted someone
who collects garbage dreams & it's all cogent
text to you. you know where this hirsute figment
sleeps when you don't, which parts of your *jiva*
it feeds on, its never spoken name. myself
i don't want to be too intimate with vague demons
that chase me in screaming impotence
toward a death that isn't there
i just want my feet to work

THE CITY POET ON THE STROLL

for Gaston Neal

my fast walking buddy slowed down
for forever he's spun 'round corners
his hustle in his bag, his habits in overdrive
too quick for the breeze; too slick for the roller

14th & u changed colors in the streaking seasons
before & after us. jellyroll, hustler to the bone
the lordly duke, swooped thru here, derbied
& spatted, wolfing on soft-hatted women
all fine in their honeyed aspect

walls of his heart, cool blow that whips
the flame, the corner's dancing gravitons
pull the brown swells home
my buddy's base spot in pittsburgh
the crawford grill, housed bebop liberated
hip boys swung out of cab's neat seats
with reet pleats into yardbird's redefined tweeds
& shades. my hip talking buddy
told stories of the pittsburgh hill: murphy men
playing on the respectable greedy. knife fights
in the pool room that didn't even stop the games
my buddy danced them to life for white
the mad painter, & me

in our new day, '56–'57, 9th & u, 14th & u
sweet & sour georgia avenue, were as swinging
as d. c. owned. some flicks in this block
latin dance in that loft, hardbop in this basement
brown bags in that cabaret, fats domino
& peg leg bates at the howard. i knew

the facades & parlors; my quick stepping
buddy knew the back rooms & alleys
upstairs at abarts buck & gus & stump let me sing on the last set
to a near empty room i like to think because the squares
had split & they thought the crowd down enough
but in truth they were tired so here, a. b., have the mike
angel eyes in c. i wanted a cool like johnny hartman's
my next buddy didn't care. he wanted to rap about the mallarmé
in my back pocket. i knew books but craved the corners
city poets from baudelaire to langston had told me of
he knew the streets but craved the books he had no guide for

        he said

so go there with me. i know hard nuance
that will decorate the rills of your brain
with glow & shadow. rooms of this limp city
where men still jam the delta blues in time
to the rimshot percussion of dice against the baseboard
know back doors to alleys where the trade
is in pleasures of the edge of the skin. the senses
order rules: you learn to see as the blind see
with the light of knowing what the books
don't teach. with the omniscient eye
of living when the power wants you dead

        yes, i said

come here with me. i know verse
that will not leave you even as the years
abbreviate memory. lines to make a family of
show you that thought you almost had
when the gray sickness enclosed you &
the scream wouldn't sound. how like the streets
the broken-line page is: you read it down
below your reason, down beneath the bottom
where mad lost truth cringes & hides

*

but the streets are treacherous in their virtue
scag poisoned my swift stepping buddy. put
a dip in his stance & a slide in his stride. snaked
a new set of veins all thru him. tracked a map
of scars 'round his now tilting form. scag
whored his love of books. bent the eye
the radical of his poems, down to corrupted
concrete earth. still my book hustling buddy
made a lyric of the stroll, sang poems of walls
made of roaches near the '64 14th & u
where the demon dooji hung

no blood humping parasite could eat my buddy
whole. i saw him build a school of pan-african
dreams where the art of struggle crossed
the bloody waters from home to home: black
flame of the burning streets, flame of the muted
poor, flame of his flaming corner. he danced
thru the crumbling walls with mad men &
mad dogs, screaming, kill martin? kill malcolm?
kill me

            we are not the only people who celebrate the death
            of our heroes by dying; are not alone in our festival
            of bones; do not sing solo before the tumescent flame
            we pantomime war in our dance of release & ululate
            "fire" in chorus at the brilliant air 'til it burns our throats
            & call it victory. we are alone in this collective isolation
            this black isthmus where i eats i & america, jailer & father
            gives us the material to construct heroes better than cities

from that time he hears the near teutonic music
of jack boots breaking the air as they descend
towards his face. no fault there. it is the nature
of jack boot wearers to abhor the cries of those
whom they have caused to hurt, to crave silence
from the voice warriors of the burning night

no fault here. my heart-first buddy hooked
the corners the alleys the readers & rappers
to the fire & sirens. brought the brown classes
to the venue of the city poem where dawn
is closure for the after-hours hustler, the moon
a lamp to work by, faith is the next vein shot
& hope is the will not to die today

my flipped-out buddy knows such madness
has value. out too far, in too deep, stability
of water, figments encircle the eye. this is
the buddy who took pound's chair at st. e's
who nursed lovers thru the deathside of suicide
who taught verse to his cellmates at lorton

       ah, but my fast walking buddy slowed down
       jewel did this. she is a dancer & showed him
       where the body ends. not at the flesh's tips
       but with the shapes embossed in air when the form
       flies away. jewel is a mother & taught him where
       the body ends. not with images stranded in space
       but at the core of her where new life curls & moves
       jewel is a lover who took him where the body does not end

the great good love slowed my buddy down

CLOUD, AS YOU

from the perspective of the cottonball cloud
that coasts above you in apparent serenity
the crooked red lightning that cracks out of it
to split the sky is not necessarily
an antonym of peace

unlike the dormant you who
makes unwelcome speeches to yourself
in that annoying retrolingual voice
from beneath all those layers
of mad choices made & deferred
that comprise you, commanding
that you stretch at last
beyond yourself, deep into
the esoteric dimension of the living
& find someplace to rest
a foot, polite conversation
with someone unlike you
some tangible item of comfort
to wear against your skin

you cark your nerves with a panic
analogous to the voltage
the cloud imparts that your ease
in estrangement will be compromised
if you evacuate this amniotic emptiness

this is how waking feels
when you sleep without dreams
a tense stasis, neither day
nor night, retreat nor advance
despite that goddamn bugle
the world blows in your ear. fall
back / spring forward
you eclipse your own light

from the perspective of the lightning
out of the belly of the seemingly
innocent cloud, you there spinning
in the vortex between thinking &
feeling & living numb are a thing
to break. it sees neither the in
nor the out of you
it only strikes

PEARL 2

Four Aperçus with Gnomic Appendices

1

pearl is frowning into her monitor
the squint of her eyes tells you she is worried
but it's her ear that's got her down
the pitch of her prose is flat. she's drawn
her people well enough: they have names
complexions, styles of dress, places to live
& go, but their voices are off key; their lyrics
do not sing. they live against their background
& not inside it. pearl can't admit that the characters
she's made have tricked her so cunningly
they've conned her into a trap that she
cannot escape: the oblique state of almost-life
where her words glance off the real
but do not penetrate it. pearl knows
that she should walk away, just back out
of these people who refuse to enflame
no matter how hard she breathes on them
o shit! she sees it now. she's in the wrong person

in first person now pearl's bopping hard
she's typed so much her knuckles hurt &
her keyboard now is blowing tunes
her people make a sort of rhythm section
under her in the way they improvise their lines
& moves: the ominous man stirs a tension
into the flow even when he's not in the room
the older woman keeps them on the one. eddie
when he enters, will be a tenor saxophone
the tessitura pearl prefers in her lovers

then ava will lean into the mike & croon
with him. their recitative will confect
into a ballad of delicate passion & staying close

writing is living strong in first person
in the revolutionary method of bebop
you make your phrases new
you swing hard thru the changes
you break down the blues

2

pearl & zaron are sitting in a gazebo
forty steps from where high tide has moved
the beach. it's pouring down rain but there are holes
in the clouds that let streams of sunlight drizzle thru
she is in loose beige diaphane; z is shoeless
& shirtless in a white linen suit that blackens
his mahogany skin. they have a jug of rum &
something between them. pearl is laughing hard, z
is conducting a story with his cigar. it is, of course
a lie, but a true one. as pearl remonstrates
with her balletic hands a slow wind blowing east
picks up their laughter & starts its
pelagic journey to the homeland shore

you can't write love if you don't have love
both parts of this truism are hard to pull off

3

pearl is in the kitchen. this is not where she lives
the lares & penates that guard her pantry
have few duties & must amuse themselves
with the creatures of imagination that she
& z emit. but there's this thing she does
with chicken breasts & mozzarella
that she's proud of & friends will be here soon
it's a housewoman moment she enjoys
for now but do not engrave this image
on your memory; pearl believes no butter
& batter can make women strong &
to commit to them would leave her issues
intact. she fears the universal sister mind
she wants to forge would etiolate
into invisibility if locked inside the home
no, she must take her causes to the page
where she can brew them & stew them
& serve them up to us

writing is wanting peace but knowing better

4

pearl & deignan are walking thru the west end's
winter funk. it's a gray day but the breeze
is soft, the magnolias' fat leaves stubbornly green
deignan is in her last trimester. d in bloom
is more femme than ever & to her credit
she remains secure in her beauty, the grand camber
of her body now laminated in that lucent skin
that glitters fertile women. pearl is humming aretha
she has stocked advice for this moment
since she carried d & is now about to break it out

but in the way of the young d thinks herself
wise. no matter, pearl will lay it on her
anyway. they smile "i know more than you think"
smiles to each other, the signature countenance
of mother-daughter love, & it is cool
wisdom, after all, is more for broadcast
than for use

which is writing: music's other voice
hummed in the key of see. writing is where wisdom
goes to sing

WHEN BLACK PEOPLE ARE

when black people are
with each other
we sometime fear ourselves
whisper over our shoulders
about unmentionable acts
& sometimes we fight & lie
these are some things we sometimes do

& when alone i sometimes walk
from wall to wall fighting visions
of white men fighting me
& black men fighting white men
& fighting me & i lose my
self between walls &
ricocheting shots & can't say
for certain who i have killed
or been killed by

it is the fear of winter passing
& summer coming & the killing
i have called for coming
to my door saying
hit it a. b., you're in it too

& the white army moves like thieves
in the night mass producing beautiful
black corpses & then stealing them away
while my frequent death watches me
from orangeburg on cronkite &
i'm oiling my gun & cooking my food
& saying "when the time comes"
to myself, over & over, hopefully

but i remember driving from atlanta
to birmingham with stone & featherstone
& cleve & feather talked
about dueling a pair of klansmen
& cleve told how they hunted chaney's
schwerner's & goodman's bodies
in the haunted hours of the silver nights
in the mississippi swamp while a runaway survivor
from orangeburg slept between wars
on the back seat

times like this
are times when black people
are with each other & the strength flows
back & forth between us like
borrowed breath

HOW FREEDOM WORKS FOR SMALL THINGS

what do you do with the lark
that finds itself somehow
trapped in your living room
desperate & confused, in panic
at its first enclosure: wall
wall, glass that looks like liberation
but stuns the beak, & now
here comes you, the biggest mammal
it's ever been near. you think
well, this is a time
when sweet reason won't work
& terror is the only kindness

so you open a window
a stressed out lark might like
the highest that you have
get a big broom & threaten
the poor bird, chase it up & up
til it finds the hole in hell
you've made for it &, free
at last, flees your happy home

hating you

OUT OF NAZARETH

1

pilate the procurator, mean bastard that he was
thought three hours a mercifully quick death
for this, what's his name? jew. he, pilate
was satisfied that he'd played the rabble well

the soldiers thought it a routine dispatch
for a slave or one not graced to be born roman

tired of holier than thou ascetics
in a town where prophets pitched gnosis
on every corner, the sadducee rabbis were smug
they dared him to miracle his broke ass
out of this one

his buddies laid low as he said they would

if the distant patriarch he called on
in the only prayer he ever taught noticed
his response was skimpy: black sky, small tremor
cracked rocks, a few crypt doors popped open
nothing major, nothing grand

2

manual for crucifixion: you prepare the apostate
by flogging. have him carry the crossbeam thru the streets
to where the stake is securely planted. a crowd
always turns out for a lynching & they will taunt him
with insults & throw refuse. let them. it makes a good show
keeps the people happy & gives the prisoner the full benefit

of the experience by letting him die humiliated. attach his feet
one atop the other to a little plank of olive wood
with a single spike & drive that into the stake. do *not*
nail the hands to the crossbeam—they will break free &
then you've got a mess. instead affix the forearms
to it. a board under the hips will hold the body up
& better excruciate the miscreant. he'll eventually die
of suffocation & if you do it right the demise
will take days. to check for the imminence of death
look for bottomless thirst, then awful shudders
of course, you could be nice & break his legs
or ribs so the shock releases him faster. *always*
stab him in the heart to make sure that he's dead
so he doesn't get buried alive. no need to be cruel

3

the marys came for him loaded with perfumes
to defend against the awful reek
of deadtown. instead they walked into a light
in the gloaming, a speaking light in the room
of the dead. speaking light that threw no shadows
in a voice that made no sound. he's not here
the light said you won't find him in deadtown
the terrible voice in the glow said to the marys
in this putrescent place of the missing dead
words in the glow of the life of the dead
shook the marys to the quick. the men
thought them hysterical

4

paul, jew of tarsus, snitch for the pharisees
fresh from the lapidation of stephen
met jesus from the foot of his horse
in a coma, blind from the light, the word
of the way in his ear, paul fell into the faith
he would make from scratch & take
to the uncircumcised of flesh & uncircumcised
of heart & out of the uptight law of moses

now off to fight the bloody bull of mithras
sweet isis, daughter of earth & sky
cybele, great succulent mother of us all
writing letters to the faithful as he went

5

celsus, pagan & proud of it, thought he'd look
into this new galilean custom: the unanimity
was impressive, & you hadda give them the morality
which was hard to come by in rome. & man
could they blow. but face it, their audience
was children & silly women, especially widows
especially widows with money, & their eloquence
was the eloquence of frogs

but who could take seriously their dictum
that the cosmos with all of its back & forth
lived in each of us? rome had it right. better
to take the gods of all nations into battle
with them. especially the ones more manly than this

THE TRUTH ABOUT KAREN

here in the solitude of distance
i see you clearer
you are carrying your mission
to the door, this time
it's stokely's last, painful year
you're saving by sculpting
a memory of fraternity
& revolution he can carry
into a champion's death in africa

now you are in your garden
amid herbs azaleas & shrubs
it is not a pristine patch
there are weeds among the blooms
i won't fatten the metaphor
of this snapshot: no esthetic
of the imperfect or seeding
of blossoms in the urban etc
it is enough that the theme
of your incessant busyness is
to find some funky thing
& make it better

even in sleep you are never still

beneath that woman
is the tender you
the one i breathe with
the passage to her opens
to the lightest touch
her transparency
in the nightlight breaks
on a soft blown kiss

i know that you better than you
she is far deeper
than her moans in the night
she is the love before birthing
the proof of the question, music
that makes the darkness live

my love, i am not a weak man
but i could not stand up
without your care. when
i'm in the bard's disgrace
with fortune & men's eyes
i call on the fool in you
who calls on the fool
in me & makes me whole

in the clarity of absence
i note that yours
is not a quiet beauty
it compels & has a radiance
we who love you stand inside of
& are home

at the top of the east a thin pink spray
behind a cloud subverts the dark
i think of you
i shave, go about my working day
my meetings are arid & won't resolve
i think of you
come home, walk our dog, observe
how timidly the tulips breach the ground
the new bird calls amid the festival of buds
in the maple trees that mark our block
& think, their songs are older south of here
where you are
i eat, hear the violations of the day
on *all things considered* & wish for you
shower, spread the lotion on my back
& wish for you. i go to bed with the radio
the sheets are cold on your side
nancy wilson sings *"i concentrate on you"*
i do
i read. the words won't hold together
perhaps tv? every corner of our house
makes ghost sounds. my sleep is thin
i dream

THE FIRST SEVENTY

in the '30s the child i was
did not doubt the wisdom & wonders
of the world or my place in it
i lived in my head
& spent my life in contemplation of wind
"rosa belle" sis minnie told mother
"a. b.'s been standing in front
of my house for an hour, looking up
in the air. i stood by him & looked
up too, but the sky was empty
no birds no planes no clouds
now he's got the whole street
staring up at nothing"
broke as we were nobody told me
there was a depression on
i learned to read & had less need
of clouds

in the '40s i had three years in the bosom
of holy mother the church & the baltimore
catechism & learned to find mortal sin
in every intuition. i toted the host
in cassock & surplice & fought
my hormones' terrible invasion
of my piousness, swung the thurible
with too much vigor as i peeped
across the censed altar at seraphic
dolores stubbs, two years older
with cherokee hair & skin the patina
of lucid midnight, on her knees
telling her beads, not dreaming
of me at all, lust-lost in my latin &
thinking the devil's thoughts with such rapture
i had to turn atheist to save my soul

my view of WWII, refracted
thru the convexity of comic books
& movies, had me seeing duke wayne
& all the caped heroes bashing nazis &
other malefactors into cross-eyed stupor
it would take me half a life to wonder
why captain america never visited
my neighborhood where my local fascists
ruled in christian unctuousness
the narrative of the times was sketched
without my image except as a priapic
chicken thieving paragon of bestial dumbness
barely fit for the back of a plow

well, stepin fetchit, snowflake
willie best, mantan moreland, butterfly
mcqueen stole every scene they entered
so give them that. give them the flair
to shine the black light with such wattage
it blurred the stars. concede to them
the grace to win when cast as lost

bebop saved the '40s. a clear wind
blew jazzbo collins into my home
from his nest in the "purple grotto" deep
in the core of the apple & in walked bud
with bird & diz & fats & monk & max
& all the cats. the sounds were faint
on my philco. i had to press my ear
against the music to assemble those cycles
of fifths, flatted to the devil's interval
those fractured chords, vertiginous changes
& bent arpeggios that swiveled around
in my head & shaped new consciousness

bebop was news that my people were moving

you can't scat bop & bow to a redneck

i got laid in the summer of '52 & went off
to howard where roi taught me cool. this was
mccarthy's d.c., jim crowed & tinted
a monumental beige, devoid of the shimmer
of art save buck & his band at abart's

howard held the moot for *brown v. board*
& hearing thurgood's homeboy gravamen
lifted my nascent wisdom to the height of a man
these off years taught me that we do walk
in the ineluctable ballistic of history
whose force will raise the worthy
in such times a people make their angels
& there at the pivot was rosa parks, beautiful
fine-boned, who rested her aching feet &
sat down on the bus that changed the route
of the world

my first were night poems: of a tree
that embosomed the moon & the fool
in repose beneath her. of wandering wet
deserted streets, staring at dark windows
wondering if these people also die. white
my mad painter friend, tried to change his style
to abstraction but found the surreal instead
if you turned his pictures upside down
the beasts of the id flew out, hunting the source
of your tranquility in edacious landscapes
just beyond your dreams' ephemeral borders
everyone could see them but white

i got laid again

in '57 i moved to n.y. & caught monk's return
from brutal exile to the 5 spot. trane joined him
on the stand with double stopping wilbur ware
no music has ever so joyously inured to itself
such explosively advancing revelation, note to
phrase, tune to set, night to ignited dawn. the ineffable
message those instruments sang to me—not the learning
we parse from text, but the meaning we feel lost & blind
for the lack of. hard & softly blown, full lives compressed
in the blazing moment of the horn
in such moments i understood the fear of art
it's in the sudden departure to places i'd never heard of
when all i came for was a little froufrou
to tack onto the dim lit walls of my consciousness
i did not hear this music so much as it occupied me
pulled me up, eyes closed to the sonic light
brain thrown hard against the back of my skull
in the sharp upward acceleration at more gees
than i could handle. my suffering silent reason yelled
stop! this air fires blue hot! there's danger in this flight
but instead my mouth gaped in the numinous yes
in the smoky dark, screamed yes monk yes trane yes yes yes

how it happened? imagine john coltrane starting the gig
enclosed in a crystal egg & thelonious dancing
the monk dance around him & trane stammering
his opening lines, a halting brilliance that did not flow
& monk dancing the invocation of swing dance
'til the line coalesced with the geometric burn
the broken sword architecture of lightning
shattered the egg in a storm of jewels
& out stepped john, wailing, this godzilla
tenor player who took me out & out & out
for the next 10 years. i have heard gould play bach
seen cunningham & fonteyn dance; known
the primal strokes of van gogh & pollock; read

the verse of the masters & all, all have remade me
but no art has so blown my inner spaces clean
so propelled me thru the stages of being
as john coltrane live. i tried not to miss a note

i often think of the sixties in mystic terms
the sweet reflective plucking of lotus leaves
in search of the jewel in the obscure heart of me
in truth it was the opposite: a desperate sprint
down the long corrupted alley to the outer self
possessing a young man's definitive clarity
i wanted revolution in america. i could see
myself in that photograph of fidel & che
in guerilla camouflage, riding into havana
on a handsome horse, smoking a fat cigar

i studied the twin mahatmas, martin &
malcolm. the south marched to
the mellifluous martin, who saw equality
as a moral state. in n.y. i heard malcolm
el haji red, for whom revolution was an act
of manhood. community was the word
of power. it extracted my jewel & appraised
its value against the notion of home
which i no longer could locate with certainty
malcolm asked me, how can you garden beauty
in your weed infused ether when your people
are firing the streets in the quest for justice?
was home the society of artists, my first cohort
of the mind? was home those depressed acres
where my race had been herded, the inescapable ghetto
of no hope with a hammer? was home the romance
of africa whose kings' legends were as grand
as arthur & charlemagne? i had a son to this
conflict, named him malcolm, & wronged him
more than i have ever wronged with my choice

i chose a home in that world of interdigitating
genes of brown memory that bound us, less by
the deathstench of the middle passage than by
the songs we made in field & factory to get us thru
my choice of commitment was karen &
the southern struggle. her tribe was sncc
& if they owned fear they burned it for fuel
alabama, mississippi—hear the cadence
of those names. they drum the accents of assassination
in the swamp, of hooded nightriding baby
blasters. the sncc folk brought a courage to the backwoods
that my father's age would have recognized as madness

karen & i made toyin, whose music i have told
you of, & kaji, whose poem i have not yet written
in the duality '70s as we watched our movement
fade. the *colored in the rear* signs were down &
the targets misted opaque. marvin gaye emigrated
from *"what's going on"* to *"let's get it on"*
i hid in the poolroom from the bougies
learned to play one-pocket from junebug
& bank from lagrange shorty. elmo
said my eye was so good i could see a hair
on a gnat's ass but he beat me for $40 that day

my hair unbraided was 6 inches tall & my clothes
were illustrated. ah quiana. your flowers are faded now
your forests defoliated, their pacific fauna stripped
of their lovely orange fur. but the power rules
in blue & gray & would tolerate no flair & so the '80s
never came. the wealthy bought them wholesale
remember the slogans: the revenge of living well?
let them eat ketchup? he who dies with the most toys
wins? remember art as corruption? benign neglect?
an empty man with a vamp's smile ruled us
& we earned him, for our offerings were lame &
our struggle slack. even music lost its heartbeat

my life distilled into the amniotic succor
of mundane love: the electrical affection of a wife
who learned commitment in dangerous struggle
the option of my son's screenplay
the lachrymose esthetic of sonatas well played
by my teenaged daughters

my work was paper & procedure, two walls
from making art & i learned the process
of compromise that auden tells us
aging is. i wrote no poems for twenty years

here, at the end of centuries, at the millennium's close
i am running from the chiliasts who stalk the antichrist
in verse & painted line. i will make no more children
but i have my poems back. they tell me to accept
that i am another lingering man, alive in the subjunctive
obedient to the law of the crossroad of time flesh
& spirit, the cadences of the tensions & releases of art
& history, the mutable landscape of trails made & litter left
surely some of this must be gift; perhaps some might be
monument as well. tell my gravestone when you see it

ORIKI

for the birth of Kaji, twenty-five years late

after Kathleen Raine

into your ear i sing a name
& from that name there runs a line
& on that run ancestors chant
the elders dance, they build to you
from their mantra a rose exhales
a summer scent to cover you
within you there uncoils the line
woman to man to first made child
to horizons beyond my sight
where settling light enwraps the cold
& in that light two hungry souls
combine combine to dream your name
& in their dream their love makes you
then from you there combusts a shout
around that shout there turns a ring
a stomp propounds a jubilee
in jubilee the ancients teach
a people rise, a people fall
we fall & rise & each new hand
will sculpt the shape of all the world
you have that force, it fires your smile
it fires your fury, fires the song
i sing to you. that you can *be*
is miracle enough for me

Oriki: Among the Yoruba, the first sound a newborn
child hears is an elder singing its private name to it,
along with the legend of its lineage.

TOYIN'S SOUND

my first daughter
was home yesterday
she seems well
she's cut her hair
to a short bush
it helps you know
her eyes

she seems well
her music flows
ever easier. i thought
it perfect before
but now she's smoothed
her oboe's small angular
sound to the mature warmth
of aged granadilla
it's a chest tone now
it's double reed
a modal implant of the orient
in the ear of the west

her voice is in the making
of those reeds. hands
she's trained so carefully
to flutter keys
carve & scrape
the cane. she runs a scale
curses, whittles, runs
a scale & starts again
until the tone
is precisely her

curious, this way
of making music
unlike the piano
or saxophone or drum
or violin. it starts
with the way she shapes
the wind
          wrong
it starts with the way
she shapes the reed
that shapes the wind
until the oboe sings
in toyin's voice

soufflé light
in its richness
a depth
she'd be too shy
to offer you
in words

*

back in chicago
the mozart *adagio*
for english horn arranged
for the same chamber
band that gil evans
spread out behind miles
on *sketches of spain*

this is toyin chanting
the evening poem
at winter's end
in the slow-blooming city
mozart has drawn this image
from that hidden cortex
at the center of solitude
where edgeless memory
composes
the soul's summation

the holy call it holy
for it is contented
to be eternal
toyin's rubato rhymes:
twilight music bridging
the lights
of the rufous sun &
the brilliant moon

her horn
is toyin's deep voice
singing thru my silence
i inhale her sound: i
breathe it backwards
till the song sings me

ORIGINS

eve rose first
saw her skin
matched the claret
mud of the riverbank
thought "i am
the first of firsts"
stepped out
to touch the day

        tall among the wildebeest
        & the placid lion
        in the one-month shade
        of the baobab
        adam stood
        observed the mating race
        of the cheetah
        the cruel pattern
        of zebra on zebra
        the wine skinned eve
        . . . & felt his blood

in the conversation
between innocence &
nescience
eve & adam considered
the notion
of life: this food
this body, mammalian
birth at the baobab
root, what to do
in sunlight
what to do
in darkness

days tumbled out
of days; the quiet waters
of night eroded
the moon's mutant
shapes. one by one
eve & adam named
the elements
of their neighborhood
but could make no word
for their greatest find
this magnetic elevation
above a world
already new

what do the newborn see
when they have never seen?
knowing nothing
they knew more
their virgin news
found on their knees
in the mating fold
of lion cheetah zebra
by remnants
of light / blinking forms
of shadow in the tepid breeze
beneath the baobab

       what the mind conceals
       the heart reveals
       love lust friendship
       trust, indistinct

in a nation of two

ON HEARING GONZALO RUBALCABA AT BLUES ALLEY

Prelude

among the things i must have known
but have now forgotten is the skill of waiting
the room looks beaten, used, abused
as a good jazz club should. voices
unattached, waft away from the discipline
of words to feed my agitation
there is vague music on the sound
system. it does not help me. my seat hardens
i squirm, i wait, i write. art will be here soon

First Tune

gonzalo is at the piano. a small sturdy man
all in black in the muted haze. i think
he is shy & will not speak all evening
except to name his bass & drum
his first chords fold back into themselves, spare
& new, abjuring the metronome. he knows
we know his flash & wants us to learn his silence
brushes on the snare lift a drive
into the tune while gonzalo hangs out at the back
of the beat where prez & billie lived, rolls around
in every chamber of the beat, at home

Second Tune

i knew he would throw it. all those years
of czerny wrapped in salsa inside bebop
swing him beyond convention. swift families of notes
sprint by in hard rhythms. right hand
firing threes left hand crushing twos & fours
i spot a candle
thru my neighbor's gin. its glow falls down
with the blues. bud powell knows you, gonzalo

Third Tune

meditation on the run

Fourth Tune

that's a sunny day. some restless *djin* inside the crowd
cannot abide soft & slow. it sounds like opportunity
to them. the conversationalists confuse quietude
with vacancy & rush to fill this new reflection
rubalcaba values so. they drop their mutter
into the deep blue rests he has made for us
a vitiation of a moment as close to sacred as i know
the way to & i must now listen thru their voices
to his invocation. (but the song! how much for the song?)
thoughts so tender they can only be sung. rhyme in the nursery
said at the bottom of my father's voice in the last sweet
instant before sleep. (*that* song: how much
for it?) long slow unpunctuated lines drift on the barest breath
(how much (the whispers break thru) for the goddamn song?)

　　　　　ah gonzalo, this is where we live
　　　　　making lines, building space, hoping
　　　　　the natter will leave our silence alone

NOTES ON A POEM: SUMMER (VERANO): CÉSAR VALLEJO

césar vallejo takes one look at summer
this lavishly berobed cleric who seeks
him out, & splits. it's a pointless call anyway
everyone has departed his, vallejo's
soul & all the jewels of july won't call
them back. but what's a sacerdotal season
to do if the soul it sought to wrap
into itself is vacant & will not be blessed?
compassionate césar has placed a rose
in autumn for summer's consecrated tears
to water. be careful says the poet
to the season, weeping upon the metaphors
of death might stir the graveyard stones
to life & then where are you? just trust
that autumn rose to live & die & live again
it always has / it always will

REDEMPTION SONG

These songs of freedom / they're all I ever had
Bob Marley

they say vuyisile mini, whose name's
a lyric, pinioned & wan, went
to the noose with a smile on his lips
& assault in his eyes. they hung him
for a song but they couldn't hang the song
zulu sotho tswana xhosa sang it
in impeccable thousands voice choirs
"look out verwoerd / black people
gonna get you" in four-part harmony
on the train to the city
at the lorry stops, the markets
in the kitchens of the boers. "look
out verwoerd" in the mines, bass
choirs in robben island prison
everyone's voice knew where to go
& it felt like joy
"we're coming for you"

they danced the toyi toyi to it
on the marches, dance that lifts
the shoulders 'til the body follows
then the knee cracking stomp
& it felt like joy. on your face verwoerd
"black people gonna get you" thru
the picture post card valley whose hills
multiplied the chord they skipped
the shebeen steps of the phatha phatha
before they turned to face the guns
"look out. beware." even when their song told
of the death of a hero it felt like joy

when the boers had torn the spirit
of soweto & time itself seemed
made of mud the children stood & sang
"no, we'll not be taught in afrikaans"

& after the revolution in song, after
the ululated lyric had freed mandela
to dance his way to the balcony above the millions
there were not streets enough or hills
enough the clouds not high enough
to hold all the song

& when they opened the pauper's grave
to retrieve vuyisile's bones they sang
no threnody at all but clicked the song
a smile creates on its way to the noose
"look out, look out" in the skeletal
tenor the wind blew in seamless sound
thru the bone-toned flute
& it felt like joy

ANOTHER LOVE SONG

dread is the hook & it hooks into us. & the walk
among our brothers twists the thing
makes an attitude of nearness that never lets us truly laugh
or truly love or truly rest
at peace. it is a subtle distress, this fear that we are the hook
of our brothers: that they know
the good things we are not, the foul things that we are
hook so deeply caught the brothers hurt
inside us, all fetus-bent & pointed to the heart
the rhyme they rap is the pain that breaks our voice
it shouts from our center, shouts from the face
reflected in the spilled blood at the foot of the stoop
we are the brothers, fear us

on the corners the brothers strut their dread
before the electric glass where the gold of the age
brays its concupiscent might. this lush dread sports
golden hair that mimes the sun
wears a thong & drives a slick car. this whore
eidolon fucks us dry & claims we'll never die
of its fatal sensuality. love this dread & know the hook
of the pipe & the spike

our america, an upas tree we camp below, drips
its milk of dread upon us, waves a star-spangled
dread in the lie of justice. it offers just enough to tease
the brothers: see? we bust no more
than a third of you, kill but the déclassé among you
the rest, you fair & schooled ones, are free
to crawl the length of your leashes on your carpets
& hardwoods, in your beamers & silks

the brothers lovingly dread america as she lies
laughing, naked, behind the glowing glass, gives
the hook a post-coital twist from her perch on our rods
for what can be more freak than to cum
to your murder? how can she not laugh in her slow
drag to our soul's vitiation, fondling
her bikini bones thru the living glass? she laughs
when the brothers thank her for the dance
thank her for the fuck thru the crystal condom
thank her for our death, & name it just
the brothers did, yes, bring the music to the party, did
teach the hiphop moves to the bone dancer
did write the lyric to the backbeat lust, did name the sisters
mere meat for the bone. their reduction
is the love song to the golden-haired thong thing
that shimmies behind the electric glass. such lust
hones the hook in the heart, fills the spike, lights the pipe
(here a press roll to the bump & grind)

& the sisters dread the brothers' bone lust popping
on the streets. it is procreant but hates a home
the sisters love love, the slow walk thru the years,
the near warm spot beneath the covers
every single night, the whispered yes that confirms tomorrow

true deep humming love of the sisters is the dread hook
answer. the hook fills the heartspace where
the sister ought to rest. she will circle in
if we clear a place for her. say yes to the dance
toward forever with the strong brown woman

remember:

they sent us moses. but which moses did they send?
not the militant thaumaturge who blast locusts
fire & death at egypt 'til the chains broke, not
the moses of the long march, the hand
of the yahweh who drowned horse & rider
the mouth of yahweh, lord of the beaten & torn
see him with his arms raised roiling the sea, looking
like john brown, the son of thunder
the terrible moses we needed but had to make
ourselves only to see them kill him as malcolm
& again as martin. no, they gave us moses lawbringer
him of the burning bush & the rules
for us alone. moses with the god voice
commanding "yield." unbending moses
of the staff of judgment who would discipline our souls &
they sent us jesus. (bereft of faith i do not clasp
his intervening invisible cosmic hand. have
no sight thru the metaphysical eye or dream
of unending life past life. but if the enduring voice
of jesus calls the brothers to the act of holding
'gainst the crush of empty gain, i will honor it)
but what jesus did they call? not the sharp
nappy-haired semitic jew who threw the shekels
in the street & chased the usurers from the temple stoop
they sent gnostic yeshua, abstract moralist
whose mission was cool with the way things were
this blond swedish looking theocentrist
with the plaintive eyes bent up & out of this world
who taught it would all get better when you die
not the militant ascetic whose primacy of the
poor both sadducee & roman thought seditious—no
they sent us gethsemane jesu, lord of the knees
whose yoke was easy & whose burden was light
not the cristos of jeremiah who fed the poor &
hated the rich but the jesu of aquinas
who hovered out of reach of culture & beamed

rays of glory down on us. matthean jesu
who fed the poverty of the spirit & let the belly bloat
who preached that meekness in this life
would earn us milk & honey
in the gold paved streets of heaven forever
such afreets devil the brothers in the dread
intersection of eternal & diurnal where the bone lust
breeds. we ply the power that beats us down
upon the sisters when no dick is scepter enough
to proclaim a brother pharaoh. the brothers fly
to the cross face first where our spent flesh awaits
the feast of the dread bone ghost

& dread is the hook & it hooks into us

ASTROLOGY

just back from eternity she applies
to the indifferent bijouterie
of the upper night for the comfort
no hand has given her. would she accept
a hand? she thinks she would
but never has. hand, sky
any consummate deed thing or being
to confirm her sapience beyond the paltry fact
that she was here to ask the question
"is there perhaps some worse state
than alive?" not quite ready to settle
for so bare a living she asks the stars again
is certain that they answered
is uncertain what they said

the weight of all this nothing
the imminent prospect of unbecoming
has made a harlequin of her
on the chance that she might catch
her painted grin laughing back
in a passing window & crack up
at such silly profile, that laughter
lust or some other art would seep down
to that deep cellar where the good wine's
stored & libate these blues away

o stars o moon o runes of night
o spirit wine o blues
know *something! know something! know!*

but what of the proximate night
whose amative intimacies the body holds?
friends, home, that kind of theatre
still playing on this side of shadow
they have light with them too
but no! those mysteries are solved
& do not answer now
they are too much the life
the life too much the cause

to stare out of the self
into this picayune globe of feckless trust
she throws her eye into the speckled dark
& stacks its minute revelations
one by one in hope that they'd compose
into useful discovery &
scans the cosmic lines in hope
of parsing this untransposed vacuity
with what she thinks to be
the cold distant wisdom
on the roof of night, the cryptic script
of the only god she knows

DEATH POEM

we in our frailty paint death
in black unspeaking mystery
the inexorable terrible wonder

we run in mark-time terror
to escape. the dead
must know that life is more

the question; death the answer
the living cannot learn. i would
ask them what the living know

of life? that life is made of love
itself insensitive to definition
too easy to say, too difficult

to mean, too hard to sort
the truth of when need is
the breath of its saying

yet our most frail & vital
aspect rides love to love's
belly where it swells & swells

seed to root, bud to fruit
the swinging heartbeat's 4/4 syncopation
in the glorious arch of the womb

we know the living heart may
not sequester from the newly
born that fragile center

that reason reserves from lovers
for the reconstruction it must do
after those vile rendings

when passion deliquesces into tears. o
but the life we build together flourishes
apart from us, a greater making

than art or news. we can shout yes
to it in its distant mirror
or dance with it squeezed to our chest

as the heart's polyrhythms drive
the silent melody the living harmonize
when they do / if they do

we know birth itself is a greater
question. this death of death is a gift
to whom? i think to the makers

who empty & fill in the cause
of renewal, who flow to the form
who enflame to the new. but how true

a gift is life to the newly born
when the only love we can pledge
is our own? all we can give is hope

that this new heart will find a heart
to ride. that it builds itself in the world
& is not built by the world

that it loves & is loved

2

& what do the living know
of death? we confuse death
in the mirror with our failings

of the hour: how we do not shine
always but sometimes dim the light
but death shines too. it is not true

to its symbols, for death is made
of bright memory. death's craft
is absence, immediate & binding

we see death as that spectral house
we must never enter that awaits
us at the turn of every corner

we fear that its chambers will be
empty & the vacant loves that once
sustained us will not receive

us there. but death is naked
of all form & does not inhabit
darkness. those few life travelers

who have peeked inside its open door
tell of a calling sun of a light
that signs the simple question

was it worth it? all those sprints
& stalls, did they make even a wind a
breeze a breath? asks with a nodding peace

that is the smile 'round nothing
of the sitting buddha's still-shut eyes
it is not death who throws terror

at every aspect of our living
the awe of its ubiquity so great
we build whole gods to dispel it

no, that is the work of the living
as the dead say only silence
in their knowing glow

A HOME BREW (1960)

the flesh of the apple. if it was,
simply, a gnawing of the flesh
of the apple, i would be talking to you
from outside you, & the images would come in simply
as voice, or hot breath blown
into your ear.

but my voice must come as your own voice,
raging between your two ears, listening
to themselves. nothing could be said there
you wouldn't have said earlier, in a stricter
voice, as, *that* fire would rage
anywhere.

the stain in my face when i talk to
you is the shadow of the woman you
love, & have. she affects the skin, as you'd say
from the core of the apple, & hold
in your mouth to ferment.

for what other image is possible
here? but a strong wine of a woman
aging on the tongue.

i say it with your voice, my tongue drunk
independent of my head. all force should move
forward, like a knife / in a quiet explosion.

A THEFT OF WISHES

the window is
                    stuffed with news
paper, sufficient
                    to hold out
side the
            undesirable
                        elements of
the outside
            but let in no
                        light. this
is what faces
            me, eternal
                        dusk, where
only the blurred
            words of
                        teleplays sifting
through the newsprint at
                        the window
                                    & an occasional
spanish
            voice in the hall
                        reminds me
                                    there's a world out
side, about
            to explode; behind me,
                                    2 impatient lovers are
whispering what they care
                        to do, in a crib too small to
accommodate
            talking . . . a good
                                    fuck would split open the
walls. home they say, repairs
                        the spirit. home is

where i never go.
           home
                is where we make
                      our noise.

there is in the atlanta
sncc office a herman bailey
poster of a brother
with his arm raised up
shoving a fist into
a turbulent sky
                        arm twice
as long as his torso, fist
as large as his head, face
on the head lost behind the
bicep. all movement is in
the arm, reaching up
to where the clouds
are at war
                the meaning
is clear. siqueiros similarly
foreshortened the fist
of an indian until it absorbed
arm, torso & countenance
                                swallowed up
the man & the scene he moved in.
the meaning is
faces look and ponder,
feel too much, are
fronts, targets for fists
                        heads
are where our thoughts circulate
confusedly, ricocheting around
corners like lightning
encased. in the streets heads
are landing platforms for the
oppressor's nightstick
                        but bailey tells us

they have heads with faces too. & you
can swing an arm, fold a hand into
a fist. you can

        bust a racist in the mouth.

in the morning part
of evening he would stand
before his crowd. the voice
would call his name &
redlight fell around him
jimmy'd bow a quarter hour
till mccoy fed block chords
to his stroke. elvin's thunder
roll & elvin's scream. then john.

then john. *little old lady*
had a nasty mouth. *summertime*
when the war is. *africa* ululating
a line bunched up like itself
into knots paints beauty black.

trane's horn had words in it
I know when I sleep sober & dream
of sun & shadow, yet even in the day john
& a little grass put them on me clear
as tomorrow in a glass enclosure.

kill me john my life eats
life. the thing that beats out of
me brews in a vat enclosed
& fermenting & wanting it to explode
like your song

        so beat john's death words down
        on me in the darker part
        of evening. the black light issued
        from him in the pit he made
        around us. worms came clear
        to me where I thought I had been
        brilliant. o john death will
        not contain you death
        will not contain you

THE BEAUTIFUL DAY X (2020)

for Bob Thompson

didn't he ramble? he rambled
rambled all around
rambled through the town
he rambled till the butcher cut him down
traditional new orleans backline song

his painter's hand reaches out
to the forest of the streets
his good beasts rush into scenes
whose inhabitants don't want them
as they do not know their needs
piero's sheba freezes in adoration
of the holy wood while bob's bird
with the man's face hovers over her
like the roof of a tent

poor harried sheba
she'd have called him a buzzard
& chased him away had her eye not been full
of the stake of jesus
& the horses that mounted the trees
that surround her &
nipped at the ladies in imitation
of voltaire's monkeys

o sheba / look around you / god's free
in the woods & he's doing odd things
ramble a little most slandered of queens
the unbroken meat of us wants to open
to a space where light flickers & flares
& nothing dances but the flame

oooo didn't / he / ramble?
he rambled

he opened up his pores to the music
he moved inside of fickle as the day
bluegrass / blues umbilically fed
east third street hardbop
downed with a straw
rhythm & blues force-fed with a spike
rude sounds sucked up a hubbly-bubbly
snort flamenco / bel canto
his very last breath

so much music his heart moved over
& death in her slick disguise
eased into the gap seductive
as the snake in the tree
she slid into his sheets
placed her mouth upon him &
with the thirst that empties
the deserts of cities
she drank his breath away

o didn't he ramble?
he rambled

THE VAN GOGH SUITE

after Steven Naifeh and Gregory White Smith

VAN GOGH IN ENGLAND

the mad mute pilgrim in van gogh
dreamed always of roads & pulled him
toward he never knew what
so he named the object of his quest "it!"

.

vincent read bunyan & carlyle on pilgrims
but it was kempis' Imitation of Christ
whose phrase swallowed him
"rejoice in misery" "in misery rejoice"

.

at three miles an hour he walked from ramsgate
to london & on in all the queer weather england made
his shoes tore up his clothes were rags
he looked untamed he must have stunk

.

van gogh saw the city on a hill at every turn
but never found a way to enter as one cursed truth rose
inside him: he had walked into the state of alone
which neither vincent nor his pilgrim could exalt

VINCENT & THE STORM IN RAMSGATE

have you seen the yellow sea
age to gold as it approaches the shore?

thin lines of light gray to black
within the gravid clouds
here's the wind / there will be storm

it is the weight of darkness that pulls
the caul & sends the vicious rain & wind
the militant agents of storm to scream
into the hawthorne blooms
that shudder with the wallflowers among
the bulwark stones & there
just past the ripening corn
trembles ramsgate

ah
the new dawn's larks riff
with the nightingales that trill their way
to nests in the gardens by the exhausted waters
for the ancient lighthouse
the storm was just another thursday with attitude
yes a star will bring you home tonight
yes there is a ship to coax to dock
yes the wet cobblestones will mimic moonlight

o god
bless me for my mother's sake

o man
do not dispute with me about the color of the waves

"not an attractive boy
hair stood up on end
homely freckled face
crooked mouth
[his family] did not know what to do with the boy
drowsy at work
wooly
rough
nervous hands
a putterer
when he had to give ladies . . . advice about the prints
he paid no attention to his employer's interests
but said explicitly & unreservedly what he thought
of their artistic value
futureless
[hanging prints in his rented room] he drove nails ruthlessly
into the good wallpaper
lived like a saint
frugal like a hermit
ate like a penitent friar
strict piety was at the core of his being
always alone
singularly silent
he had no intercourse with anybody
charming strangeness
a queer fish
not like a normal man
out of his mind
cracked
needs a jolly heart"

the borinage was the black country
for coal & the comprehensive refuse of coal
coal air coal dust black water
toxic soil indelible serpentine tattoos
etched by coal into the skin of the miners
slag heaps posed as mountains against the horizon

they called the coal-blackened women "false negresses"
even after the "denoirissement" of their baths
ancient children who snaked through crevices
where coal veins hid were never seen to smile

*

vincent
cleaned and pressed for once
arrived in the borinage
foolish
& departed mad

his guidebook image of the borin
was that they sang
their way to & from
the mines
praised god in blessing
as they cut their bread
he would be their catechist

but the borin were so whipped
they envied the pit horses
that lived their entire lives
in the steaming offal
of the earth
for their constant oats
& clean straw

*

vincent preached
why are you resentful?
yes death hides everywhere
in the mines but where
does death not hide?
death is the route to heaven
be glad of its imminence

he renewed his pilgrimage
at the bottom of the earth
past the pit head "up in hell"
rode the cables down a chasm
so deep "the daylight . . .
at the top of the shaft dwindled
to a spot as small as a star in the sky"
stooped his way through barren tunnels
in water deep enough to flood his boots
crawled through flammable air
into tiny cul de sacs where dismal men chipped
at veins three inches thick

vincent preached
why whine
about your fourteen-hour days?
to the marxists who would have you strike
say jesus was like me "a workman with lines
of suffering & sorrow & fatigue on his face"
be like him
rejoice in misery

the borin thought that the dumbest shit
they'd ever heard

*

did you unearth your madness
in the black pits vincent?
that day the mine blew
did the vestiges of your sanity
erupt in satanic flames &
char to dust the sorting girls &
the pick ax men & the saint
you'd learned you never were?

but you nursed
survivors angelically
it was the best of you
we ever saw

*

mortify vincent
abjure the sinful
vanity of the bath
eat stale discarded crusts
rag your clothes again
go barefoot through winter
sleep in the hay & wake up
crusted in frost
rejoice in misery vincent
mortify

VINCENT IN LOVE 1: KEE VOS

(Vincent:)
i've decided
i will love kee vos

my father dorus'
church is all over me
it's in my beard
in the nap of my tweed
in my shoes
in my eye
i can't be dorus
without a wife
i've decided
i will love kee vos

(Kee Vos:)
what does
the village creep
want of me?
i swear something fell
that wants to suck
the marrow
from my soul
stares out at me
from those recessed green eyes

(Vincent:)
"a man cannot stick it out
in the open sea" alone
cousin kee you are bereft
& i am lonely
to be respectable
i require a wife
we share a misery
with god's own son

& that is warmth enough
i've decided kee vos
you will give me the love
your husband died under

(Kee Vos:)
my husband just interred
& this freak wants my hand?
he will support me
with salable art?
he compares
his babbling letters
with lark song
& writes of love
as if it were a bulb
one buys
plants in autumn &
harvests in spring
"never never no never"

(Vincent:)
i am expert
at losing myself
in the gauzy environs
of rampant imagination
boundless & sliding
downward
toward a ruined bliss
that releases me to
all the hurt
that absence brings
this i name love
if it's derangement
i answer to derangement
to the dementia
of the unloved lover
who can't take love
because it will not cower

kee my right hand
cooks on the wick
i will char it to the bone
if you do not come to me

i have drawn sien hoornik in left profile
nude & seated no huddled on a stump
                                   her arms are wrapped
around her face to hide the smallpox scars
from you who are callous enough to stare
at so pitiful a form
                         the back of her head
peaks above a dead horizon
life is scant around her

sien's back is bent & warmed by greasy uncombed hair
the long black nipples that i love dangle to her thighs
where a belly roll supports the wide black aureoles
that pride deserted long before this thirty-third year
her elbows rest upon her knees
                                   the hand
that emerges between arm & thigh
portrays a failed strength

this is a body whose force was depleted
by half a life of tricking on the streets
of the hague
                   by the children
she cannot love
                   by the clap
she shared with me
bad liquor cigars & the street worker's syntax
that sanded her voice to a scraping growl
are enwrapped in those arms
                                   no i will not show you
her face for you will not see the same sublime image
that i recognized as delacroix's *Mater Dolorosa*
you will not see the sacred virgin who
cowers within the folds of this ruined woman

sien's virgin
        do not despair
                i house a dormant pilgrim
he will rescue you

VAN GOGH IN ARLES

Dear Theo

locked away
i have found my freedom
in this asylum i am safe from the arlesians
who threw stones & horse pies at me
as i sketched them on the streets

paul is gone
he was supposed to deepen my eye
lengthen my view give reach to my name
instead gauguin has taught me
that lunatics are better company than artists
they know more see deeper & never turn away
if only they would learn a softer midnight scream
did he ever claim the half-ear i left for him
with the pimp at the brothel door?

at last i have a community that lives with me
in the unexalted state of alone
from which i paint & write to you

the air here is thick but clear
the gardens are true in their wildness &
filled with sympathetically gnarled forms to draw
my mind now knows that it is lost
& so my sight is free to catch the abstract
twisted motion of things & beings at risk
i send to you now *The Roots* which holds
these shapes & *Cypresses* whose green leaf flames
are like the poplars i shipped before

theo this rich night sky combusts all over
the crescent moon goes yellow
to teal to azure with the planets &
clouds that swirl their ballet for me

dear brother you well know my love
for women is more dense than renoir's
for i do not see them as lit from within
to some milky purity that never catches dirt
their beauty is lustworthy
hard life cuts as many furrows in their faces
as it does in mine
some days i think the impressionists wrong
the world is more than placid light
i tell you theo i tried pointillism
but the colors of the day
do not blend harmoniously or decorate
each other into glorious songs
of sight as seurat preaches
they wrestle & thrash wage war & mate
with a cacophony i swear i can almost hear
still gauguin wants a constant image
that neither starts nor finishes
monet wants no texture to his surface
to corrupt the feather touch
that spreads his sun upon the pond
degas dreams vermeer & his glassine canvas
oh i know how stratified his surface is
glazed wet on dry at six levels
but damn edgar show us what roils you
scream the image man
they all want the anonymous brush
but there's a burning truth
in my impasto for it lets my pilgrim work
his desperate hand into the stroke

clear pristine light is blindness theo
the flames are all

that's what the others missed

SELF-PORTRAIT, 1887

this
    my face
describes
the mythic tragedy
of mirrors

i have set my portrait
in the expressive gestures
of the brush
                no flat space disputes
the inherent violence of sight

i did not pretend it was god's surface
smooth & clean & classic like degas'
but laid it enlever
           mottled
so no moment of your inspection
is serene

this face was not crafted in thoughtful sequences

nothing is tranquil
not my rough wool coat not
the leopard-skin background
not the blaze that spreads from my beard
to my lobe & up into the hair that i cut myself
there is a nervous light
across my forehead that dims its way
down the line of my nose
where the inner conflagration the nostril vents
soon will set my head on fire

i have known the hell of burning
all my life but the goddamned mirror
will not let me call it peace

the topology here is parlous
a rufous absinthe mound rises
below the promontory eyebrows
to shade green viper eyes
that condemn you for the pretense
of your quietude

*

i set out to paint the eyes of a bonze
in profound meditation
but the glass could not find them
& offered mine instead
                              it knows what lives
inside those orbs & the scathing light
that flares out of them
& why they are at home
in a face on fire

Dear Theo

now that you have joined me at pilgrim's end
for love of you i surrender the privilege of silence
that is the sole reward of death
i do wish you had chosen a passage better than mine
to this boring peace / not the way of the pox
that twists the brain & corrupts its force
so you stagger blind awake or in dreams
through a war where all combatants are you

i never knew how to live so how could i have known how to die?
but i wanted a sweeter death for you little brother

who shot me? does it matter? that odious bully réne secrétan
who put salt in my coffee & snakes in my paint box?
whom I called "the terror of the smoked herring"
& who called me "the faithful lover to the Widow Wrist"
after he caught me masturbating in the woods? no
he tormented me because i was never mad enough for him
making me dead would cost him a victim

did I shoot myself behind the dungheap as some have written?
in the stomach? at distance? theo you know how dishonorable
i think suicide to be & that i would never do it by the vulgar gun
if i had to i would drown myself with elegance
with lilies near & florid japanese silks about my person
(they tell me here that death below the waves can be ecstatic)
no it does not matter who shot me theo
it matters that i did not shoot myself

i think of poor poxed-like-us franz schubert
snobbed all the way to the crypt in queer-hating vienna
that all my sorry years condense into his terminal sonata
& i am the pilgrim of that first movement who settles in the air
& guides the hopeful theme as it searches
the rounded borders of e flat major
for a foot to stand upon until all dissonance
has fallen out of the key & the questing air
must swing back unto itself if it will have purchase

that the beginning is the resolution every time

theo i have lived that theme

little brother we began in the love of the true
we were the ictus & rebound
that christens the new
the tension & release that gives soul to the image

but dear theo
not even in the grave do we resolve
& that
if i am true
is the best of us

so there you were in paris
wishing you'd arrived in time
to hang with senghor & césaire & diop
but they'd suspended poetry & gone home
to senegal martinique & guinea
to govern or nag government
to dig tunnels away from the colonials
yet there was enough negritude left
among their roiling progeny
to feed one ethiop seer searching paris
for places for your eye to settle

your luggage stuffed with image & icon
symbols designs colors shapes & sounds of africa
seen & heard from fat windows of axum & lalibela
part copt pre-rasta you with the wisdom of griots
the songs of mali polyphonic yodels of entire villages
of the ba homunculi of the ituri forest in counterpoint
as elaborate as a bach chorale & then the deep bass
harmonies of the zulu who stomped as they blew
& the drum carved from the blessed tree
& the art of benin & fulani & more all jostling
inside your trunk awaiting your application

in paris with the poets gone home

*

if one put marx & freud in a bowl & stirred
& baked for seven years would one confect
a new mind? frost with negritude infuse with juju
decorate with the 500 letters of the amharic alphabet
would that mind be brown & chant
the thunder dreams of the lost & more than lost
people of dance & drum?

*

we tour his canvas:
there is a snake as everyone respects a snake
now the snake is a river perhaps the nile
its powers are manifold & mostly benign
the landscape it describes is populated
with the transparent fauna of the master
who paints from the mind & not from the eye

now there is a bird as everyone loves a bird
her wings are flared whether she stands or flies
she flashes her potency / her image decorates nothing
i've come to know her muted song

i have her surveying a field of cracked eggs
in which a brood of cruel fell hatchlings scream
to be fed vietnamese meat
her breast sports the stars & stripes

*

i cannot write with jazz in the room
yardbird parker & john coltrane inhabit my brain
& hold it in a state of limp wonderment
far above the naked empire of words
but skunder could mambo his brush across
the canvas & swear that 'trane & bird swung
his creatures outward & filled them with the sacred juju
that great music turned up all the way cannot be loud
that's why i'd rather be a painter than a poet
but then i'd rather play a horn than be either

*

the thing about booze is that it takes
its time when it comes to enslave you
it tickles a room full of friends for you
suspends all the stress in your body
grants you dreamless sleep against
the arrogant entitlement of nightmares
booze is greedy but never could kill
the light of the juju in skunder

the thing about booze is it makes you lost
in your hours while you secretly know
that you murder yourself
the thing about booze is it loves you

*

an essay on the myth of universality:
the only thing universal in human existence
is the death that came too soon for skunder
the critic's bona fides is a begged question
that one eye can see it all & know the worth
of all art or one ear can hear what swings in all music
or even one music is epistemological imperialism
no one who listens to music close enough
to be moved by it is ever wrong no matter
how much i hate that goddamn band
the five people who guard the gate to wealth
& glory in the art plantation are smug in the eye
can see the microdots the quarks the hemiquavers
of the picture but they can't see skunder's serpent's song
even as it saturates my senses
it is because they resist that vibration in the echo
the one that tells of the ancestral africa
their forefathers saw as a mall to rape
& not a place to be humble before
the critic has no right to be wrong

*

& so sweet little man with the aquiline nose
& the paint caked forever under your nails
& the laughter brewing on your tongue
now you are among the ancestors you chanted to
senghor & césaire & diop are there to show you
the hippest spots of the perfect harlem of the stars
& your demons are left behind to commute
between your pictures & our dreams

between the night & its shadow is the music
between the music & the night is the song
between the song & the music is the voice
between the voice & the music is the self
between the self & its song is the mind
between the mind & the song is the melody
between the song & its melody is the rhythm
between the rhythm & the melody is the mind
between the mind & its song is the word
between the word & the mind is the voice
between the voice & the word is the thought
between the thought & the voice is the self
between the word & the self is the shadow
between the shadow & the self is the light
between the light & the word is the music

(the song is the melody in the word in the rhythm
the self holds the mind to the word & the thought of the song
the voice in the song sings the self to the mind
the light lights the shadow of the voice & its melody
the rhythm moves the self through the dimming night's song
the thought in the song is of night's shadows without music)

THE CONGO GOD TEACHES J. S. BACH A DANCE

after Ned Sublette

when i n'sala banda the congo god
of iron & storm left the barracoons
of fernando po all they left of me
was a tactile memory of the drum
stored in hands cuffed in my essence
the iron of my image
in the alimentary basement of a ship
redolent of piss & shit & puke
& the stale but hopeful bouquet
of death

what's a god to make of that?
what demons can corrupt
my elements this way? what demons
can lower my lovers to this?

*

they bartered gods
in the babel-mouth
cane fields of matanzas
& i got sung
as zarabanda & rhymed
with ogun of the yoruba
who too exhaled
the ferrous fire
in the dancing forests
my lovers sang to the feral tree
emptied its chest to tone the drum
left a little blood on the inside
of the skin so the drum
would house a soul

to tell my shame
to my thunder & flash
my anger on the sky

*

drum & song
splayed toes tap patterns
into black soil in the congo time
my drums spell out
at midnight worship in the deep
rain forest where
i ride my children
pump the arms chatter
the castanets swing
the hips snap the spine

post an image of the nazarene
in case the priests show up
they know too little of rhythm
to name the god inside it

*

one day i will reign here

*

at the feast of corpus christi
in havana & sevilla my children
roiled the spirits of the mob
with the zarabanda
the church thought my dance a bridge
to hell: padre juan de mariana called it
"so . . . lascivious . . . in its sway
that it was enough
to set decent people afire"
covarrubias de orozco thought my dance
so evil the jews must have created it

*

the priests were not entirely wrong
my children built iron into the drums
to set me in each cadence & i mounted
souls in every dancing crowd
my tempi set in the marrow
rose through the arteries
flooded all reason
the priests screamed "demonic possession"
& flexed their crucifixes but i
had the drum & my drum
was seditious

*

the strings from the sahel north
of congo sang my beat in sevilla
in naples over france into
the germanys in the new voice
of guitar
less evangelical
than the drum

away from my children
my chants fell out
my beat could barely move
dressed in silks & perfumed
to be presented
to the court just out
of plainsong &
wanting to dance
without a notion of swing
so they smuggled my bleached-out
sarabande through the servants' entrance
where sebastian bach found it
& called it new

IN LIEU OF NIGHTINGALES

this night can't quite
be quiet
the streets
must have their say
the parlous keens
of sirens sear
my stillness
the wind that whistles
in the window frames
the discursive
reveilles
from the halfway house
next door as the mad
folk try to scream
their way out
of themselves
are all more fugues
in evening's grotesque lullaby

a faint tremolo inside
these thelonious
chords horripilates
my spine
tells me
that nothing will be
where i left it
when i awake
the keys
to my silence
will be lost again
in plain sight
among the minute crises
that escort me
from scene to scene

hang here long
enough & it all
congeals
into a queer
presence
doesn't it?
a sad little bovine
melancholy
that is this murky
city's salient demon

i swim up
& look down
for a moment
upon the singular village
that human darkness is
even without
the unfathomable nirvana
that dreams claim
to carry

what's to be seen
inside its mythic
stillness?
the clanging paradox
that silence inhabited
is not silent
that stillness
with me in it
is never still

night
is the ear's domain
night's voice
is the shadow
that shadows cast
imperfect
& out of tune
like the rest of us

IN THIS PECULIAR LIGHT

in this peculiar light
i see no farther
than the edge
of my voice
        therefore
i assign all eternal memories
to a restless grove
a stuttering album of places
deeds & parts of you
that is vivid &
a comfort to browse
& in its own fluffy way
resolves this day

i begin to wonder
what you would perceive if
by some alice or dorothy
accident you slipped
& fell into the neon box
of crayons
that remembrance is
as it flashes its staccato way
through this peculiar light

i think
you'd wince at first
then turn away
then turn
to me
your smile would be
gratuitous
but well intended
& i'd count that
good enough

NOSTALGIA FOR THE LIGHT

after Patricio Guzman

there's not a hint of water
in the air above the atacama desert
only light older than time

time comes late among the stars
that flock to the atacama
desert to be seen
you can hear the big bang's
string tones
mark the tempi
of bursting stellae
whose supreme distance
makes a nullity of hours
among the motes of light
that dust the bones
that fill the atacama desert

every memory is buried
in the sky
above the atacama desert
the enslaved indigenes who
scooped saltpeter from the sand
the ancient herdsmen whose herd
memories are the freest here
they at least could carve
their images among the llama
into the neutral stones

call these shepherds origins
call death a theme of origin
say time & light
are witnesses to origin
that renew but don't remain

2

when pinochet delivered his pet corpses
here did he note the brilliant
night? did he see time end
in the fatal illumination
the antique carcass ghost
light of stars that died
in the time before time
before our earth was born
light that seeps into the sands
is calcified & stored amid
the shards of the disappeared
to be sorted with the tears
of the mothers who sift
time sand & light
for the reliquary bones
of their loves?

of us all these women know time
best for it is dressed
in absence & the tools
of remembrance: a photograph
the top half of a skull
a mummified foot still in its sock
& now a grotesque
mantel sculpture

time in the atacama desert
is abolished by the bones

THE MIGRATION SUITE

IDA MAE, VAN FLEET, MISSISSIPPI, 1928

after Isabel Wilkerson

ida mae's most memorable toys were
water moccasins
                    she dangled them
from the tips of sticks   tossed the snakes
into the air & caught them (on the sticks
not in her hands)

she hunted rabbits with a branch
would sneak up on a sleeping one
& whack it on the head
good eating

ida mae couldn't grab enough cotton
to fill a pair of socks or plow
a straight furrow but she cut wood
& liked killing snakes &
her father loved her for that
& for smaller unnamed things

in a diabetic coma the grownups
thought him dead but ida mae said no
he's not cold but what did a kid know
they buried him warm in the church yard

so there never can be a question of where you walk
you must get the hell off the sidewalk
if a white person approaches

elevators put you much too close to us
go to the freight lift as that is what you are

at the bus & train stations you will be in the colored waiting room
even if it costs us twice as much to maintain one

use the colored window at the post office
& call on the colored public telephone so we won't have
nigger earwax rubbing on our ears & nigger breath
laid near our mouths

if you reach an intersection before a white person
wait for the white car to go through before proceeding
& never pass a white driver on the road you arrogant bastard
any accident with a white driver is your fault as you know

never speak first to a white person or contradict a white person
or be first to offer your hand to a white person
never speak to or look at a white woman unless you want to be chopped up
& barbecued

park in the colored parking spaces across the street
if we have to drag your thieving ass to court
swear on the colored bible as the testaments
& gospels don't mean the same for you & us
god will explain this when you die & your black soul
goes to whatever garbage dump nigger souls go to

so i tell short willie "short willie you too mad
to talk to that colored-hating ofay
wait till you cool down" but you know short willie
he always swinging on some two-ton motherfucker
'scuse my french & getting a mudhole stomped
into his little ass 'scuse my french
but it's settling-up time & every year
short willie got to listen to this big no-neck peckerwood
he sharecrop for call the numbers out his book
"this much for flour that much for vet fees"
for that crazy mule poots in short willie's face
all day long damn mule won't gee nor will he haw
'scuse my french "this much for a screen door
& that much for tin & lumber for the roof
& your crop weren't worth that much
so you owe me this much plus what
you been owing me but don't you worry
i'ma still give y'all credit at the store 'cause
you & florine 'bout the best fieldhands i got
maybe if you stop wasting that little picanniny
a yourn's time in school & put him out in the field
where he belong at you might can break even"

now that's the wrong thing for that cracker to say
'cause short willie real proud of how smart little willie be
& he pick guitar good too for such a young boy
so short willie go off on the boss' ass 'scuse my french
he call that man everything but a child of god
short willie he says "every year you pull this same shit"
'scuse my french "i know i bring in the best crops
in the county & they worth a whole lot more
than what i takes out that fucked-up store you run"
'scuse my french "& you left a whole lotta bales
out the count like you do all the time

now you want me to take my boy outta school
well little willie he ain't never gon do stoop work
for no cheating slave-driving white man like you"

that's when the big redneck jam his .44
into short willie's belly all the way up to the cylinder
tell short willie "nigger how you like a hole
in your ass so big your goddamn stomach fall out"
'scuse my french "you won't be the first coon
i done skint nor the last one neither
so you best haul your black ass on down the hill"
'scuse my french "& start getting them acres
ready for next year's crop"

but you know short willie he always got to say
one more thing so soon as he got the mule
up to a gallop he holler "i ain't gon take
this shit no more" 'scuse my french
"that black ass is the last part of me you ever gon see
i'ma get my family on up outta here & you can tear
your own fingers up on them damn cotton burrs
& as long as your asshole points to the ground
don't you ever pull a gun on me again
so fuck you & the horse that brung you"
'scuse my french

now i done told short willie & told short willie "short willie
if you going just go & keep your fool mouth shut
for the lord's sake don't tell no white folks"
but short willie that little banty rooster
say he ain't scared of no cracker
& he lollygags along trying to sell off all his stuff
& running his mouth 'bout how he cuss out this white man
i mean if you ain't scared of a alabama peckerwood
then you ain't scared of a rattlesnake
& if you ain't scared of a rattlesnake
you ain't got good sense & you know short willie
sometimes ain't got the sense god gave a mule tick

everybody know you don't take the bus
from downtown where they knows you
you goes down to birmingham & takes
the illinois central up to fulton kentucky &
transfer on to chicago but that fool short willie
go to town in his sunday-go-to-meeting suit
& try to buy bus tickets
& the sheriff there waiting for him
the boss man done turned him in
the sheriff he took & charge short willie
with vagrancy or some shit 'scuse my french
& sell him to the sloss-sheffield mines
up in coalburg for ten years & split the money
with that hateful redneck short willie
been sharecropping for

you remember lee otis mincey
from over yonder in plumbnelly
used to stack the hundred pound croaker sacks
at the tater grader? sheriff sold him
to that mine & when he come out
six-seven years later poor lee otis
wasn't no more good
couldn't walk right couldn't stand straight
blind in one eye couldn't see out the other
hollered at haints & shadows all night long
with the mouth short willie got on him
he ain't coming out atall

i'm sure lord mighty 'blidged to you for driving us
down to birmingham in your nice packard
reverend bascom & don't worry i got the gas
both ways even though i thinks eight cents
is way too much for a gallon
i promised short willie through the jailhouse window
"hope god may kill me stone dead short willie
i'ma take your family on up outta here"

my sister constance she up in chicago doing real good
she say they charges negroes three times
the rent they charges white folks
but she got her a beauty parlor
makes plenty money
fixing the ladies' heads for church
florine sleeping back there
with little willie's head in her lap
she fry hair real good too &
sis' constance gon rent her a stall
& little willie he can go to school
& get him a little job
they can stay with sis' constance
help her out with the rent
constance she say i can get work
toting quarters at the meat packing plant
i'ma send for mocile
soon as i gets us a place

nawsuh reverend bascom i knows
we ain't crossing the river jordan today
chicago ain't gon be no kinda heaven

but down here in alabama a negro
got the buzzard's luck
cain't kill nothing
won't nothing die

KANSAS CITY BLUES, 1934:
COLEMAN (BEAN) HAWKINS HUNG UP

Seeing is believing, but hearing is a bitch.
Lester "Prez" Young

in '34 america partied wet again
& you didn't have to hide your booze
not that pendergast's kay cee
ever tried life dry

the Cherry Blossom
was the hot new spot
its japanese motif flashed
red & white flowers
in the wallpaper & in the kimonos
of the fine brown geishas who served
& flirted for tips
bill basie from jersey swung the house band
& when fletcher henderson & his boys
hit town they all fell by

& coleman "bean" hawkins
founder & absolute monarch
of the tenor sax
made the dauntless error
of sitting in

bean didn't know the kay cee tenors
so they lined up on his ass
                        herschel evans
hawkins' texas tenor progeny
deep voiced & blowing blue note thunderstorms
stretched him all the way out
& would not be cut
next came the mighty ben "frog" webster

a peer coleman didn't know he had
whose breathy chain of azure dreams
fell gracefully out of each other
on their way from the root to the new

& then
              o shit what swinging hell is this?
                                      lester young
sax cocked at 45 degrees
the cool voice that fired the hottest sounds
tone light enough to ride
across the room on clouds of smoke
five choruses to warm up but then
& then & then & then a new indigo lyric
flowed over the joint
without floor or ceiling
                        mary lou williams' sleep
was broken by frog webster's tap on her window
"wake up pussycat
coleman hawkins is hungup at the Cherry Blossom
& all the piano players are sweated out"
& there she found great bean in his singlet
shirt neatly folded on the chair
searching his horn for a lick
that would win this all night chase

he never found it
                  the music
never closed in '34 kansas city

KANSAS CITY BLUES, 1934: BIG JOE TURNER

the music never closed
at the sunset club near 12th & vine

as night blended into morning
big joe turner mixed drinks
at the bar while pete johnson
elaborated b flat at the upright

to the 4/4 percussion
of ice against shaker
pete tickled a chord they shared
& big joe shouted a blues so true
you remembered you'd once lived
that never ending hard love song

*

wipe the bar close the tabs
cross the street to the lone star lounge
to barter breakfast sing a funky song
with the cats jamming there
"you can take me pretty mamma
roll me in your big brass bed
then you can boogie my woogie
till my cheeks turn cherry red"
hang out gossip lie & laugh
cross back to the sunset
it's been an hour & a half
& pete's still jamming
the same blue blues
shout the last verses
take back the bar

time rolled its choruses in circles
in '34 kansas city

HARLEM: MINTON'S PLAYHOUSE

(Yeah, I know. I took a lot of liberties.)

ladies & gentlemen cats & kitties
tonight at minton's playhouse
we got the band to flip the music
from the jumping jive to the atomic groove
hooked up by our piano professor
with the mystery vonce
thelonious sphere monk
from rocky mount north carolina
walking the bass all the way
from waynesbora virgina
is red calendar
that young blood kicking the drum kit
is from newtown north carolina
which i hear is way back up
in the Great Dismal Swamp
don't serve him liquor bartender
'cause he's just eighteen years old
let's have a big hand
for max mac skibbon zout roach

wailing his ass off on the tenor saxophone
is that short man with the giant sound
from savannah georgia
he's in the mood for love ladies
give it up for james moody

swinging his way down from the stratosphere
you know the beret the horn rims
& the goatee if you don't know him
lay five on five
for cheraw south carolina's finest
john birks gillespie
known for good reason
to squares
& hipsters alike as dizzy

i ain't hip to how they all slid out
of dixie to jam up here at minton's
but could you dig these cats out in a field
grabbing cotton & shouting work songs 'bout
ain't that berta coming
down the road?
well she
looks like berta
but she
walks too slow

these studs got horns to shout with

like james moody o rooney mo
how do you fall out of savannah
blowing that much horn? this cat can blow
a line so long deep & warm
you'll want to sleep inside of it
his old lady told me he even snores in b flat

red walks his bass but if he walks it slow
it's to send that gone frame
he's got eyes for there at the front table
& max don't like to walk at all
he likes to drive & there's no speed limit
in those swinging spheres he travels through

speaking of spheres thelonious monk
ain't weird like they say
he knows weird he dances with weird
he wrote weird's theme song so it lays
just past where your ear
thinks is as far out as it can go
but he's a very hip cat
the band's gonna lay a monk tune on you
that's so far out it's in
mysterioso

*

those are the sounds
we're putting down
the new blues that brews here in harlem
blues on blues in blues

like the poet said
you got to dig it to dig it
if you don't dig it
you won't dig it

so cats & kitties
that's all the hipness
we gon lay on you tonight
remember
always be cool & go forever in vout

INK SPOTS

when i was a boy
the Ink Spots were a crossover quartet
they were black & worked in white suits
you may think of this as jim crow jovial
so securely hard core it was a chuckle all around

draw a cross line near the bottom of the page
shade in all the tones from teasing tan to authentic black
sprinkle bessie blue sweatstains over
that was us holding up the rest

their lead singer was bill kenney
a tenor whose falsetto sounded like chest tones &
whose diction was so clear you could spell
the lyrics by his phrasing
the bass was orville jones
after kenney crooned orville spoke
a laid-back version of the lyric punctuated
with his heartfelt "honey child"
a curious locution to my pubescent ear

shade the area just above us
in the dinge of poverty
this was the nightmare land
of the white poor who were taught
they were better than no one but us
so be grateful for your ignorance & remember
to decorate the pine & oak forest at the border
to whiteworld with nooses & flaming pyres

i liked their heavy songs: "we three
we're all alone / even in a memory
my echo my shadow & me" &
"why do you whisper green grass?

why tell the trees what ain't so?"
i wished they sang "Nature Boy"
but nat "king" cole owned that song

> *put all the good stuff near the top of the page*
> *swimming pools / schools with new books*
> *homes with black servants*
> *night clubs where the Ink Spots sang*

there was baseball in both worlds
& on the barnstorming fields
we skunked them
who was babe ruth to josh gibson?
cy young to satchel paige?

> *one lonely black spot stood as a whole man*
> *stands in the middle of whiteworld*
> *see jackie robinson suspended in flight*
> *above the honed spikes*
> *as he turned the double play*
> *see him steal third / see him steal home*
> *yea! yea! nigger! nigger! yea!*

after *brown v. board* told me how jim crow
bruised my mind i was ashamed
of the Ink Spots & all the accommodating
black stars like them speckled
across that strange white sky
close but impossibly distant

now i tell my granddaughters
this is what talent could not prevent
your great grandparents from living

now i try & fail to convince them
that bill kenney's high precise phrases
were good singing

JEFF'S POEMS, 3: THE SERMON

You wonder why I stand here, black in my skin
and dripping with sin
in this white folks' church.

You think that I am like you,
here in this room because I have heard
that this is where God sleeps.

But I am not. I have no use for God today
as I am empty. A polluted vacancy spreads inside me.
My shell holds a great nothing that I fill
with the scorched sugar scent of crack.

No, sweet church, I do not present a vacant temple
for the Lord to enter, for there is no thing, no one,
inside to receive Him.

And that is why I'm here.
I am looking for my soul.

For I have lost it. Lost it somewhere deep.
Deeper than my heart,
Deeper than my mind,
Deeper than my arms can reach,
Deeper than my voice can scream,
Deeper than my eyes can see.

You cannot know that place.

Can you search the hollows of my heart?
The pipe has stripped it bare.
Can you search the vast and empty caverns of my mind?
The smoke has scorched it black.

Crack has looted the best of me
and I have nothing to give this daughter of Africa,
at my right hand,
this son of Ifa at my left.

Somehow I weigh more without a soul to lift me
as this nothingness pulls me down.
I am fixed to a barren ground
even though my roots have come undone.
The Lord of psalms does not enter where I live
as the crack absorbs my prayers.

Oh Reverend, Oh pastor, Oh horn above the pulpit
I have no soul to offer God.
Even Satan does not want me.
There are none like me among the scriptures.
No testament for the crack-head fool.

If you can sing my soul back to me
please sing it.
If you can pray my soul back to me
please pray it.

Please help me find my soul again
so I can look for God.

Brief years ago he saw how crack ate his step-dad's soul.
Now on the 1 Train to music he saw the ruined man asleep,
greasy clothes all slack,
in the slump of one whose spine has left him.
Where was the sculpted bulk that used to stretch his shirts?
His feet were bare in the late fall chill.

Should he speak?
For stop after stop after stop
he searched his mind for questions
that were not written
on the corpus of the disappearing man:
How are you?
Dying.
How have you been?
Dying.
Where do you live?
I do not live.

Ashamed of his shame,
he stepped off the train and tapped the window.
The wan ghost startled.
How are you? The ghost pantomimed,
How have you been?
Where do you live?

CHANDI DREAMS OF BUTTERFLIES

last night chandani dreamed
of butterflies settling in her hand
at three in sleep she skips
through the invisible glens
of jackson heights & lifts
from space the petal winged
creatures of air & stem

her near-first word was "moon"
she knew it from the book
& marveled for hours
that it balanced above her
the light in the night

she tells me of her dream by skype
from beneath the comforter
on her mother's bed as she deploys
her princesses against the day
toyin
        almost forty
                        whose dreams
i used to know
shares this snuggle cave with her

there must have been a time when
my dreams were innocent flicks
of flowered creatures
that fluttered above my palms
i must have discovered one night
the moon & all its mutable geometry

now in sleep i am often lost
& afraid
my dreams are polluted
with demons chandani
has not yet met
some are political & despise me
as i despise them for the warring
worlds we want to make
others are the seepage
of the latent madness that waits
till midnight to claim my mind

i would not dream for chandani
i'd have her dream for me

CAELI EMERGENT

dearest caeli

behind the many crooked faces
i threw at you to get a drooly laugh
i thought
this gorgeous neonate
has no sense of humor
or maybe old guy jokes only work
on old guys

it was my way of asking
for an interview with one
who had so recently screamed
her way out of the womb:
please tell me of the amniotic
comfort of the sacred sac
what did you hear in there? did
you hear your father play guitar?
did you hear your mother sing
& think "this is the song
whose belly i ride?"

most of all please report
your wombside dreams to me
with what material did you make
dream images when
you had never seen shape
shade tone line or depth
much less the colors of the day
was there a narrative
in your theatre of sleep?
were you both figment & theme?

& what womb experience
taught you to withhold laughter
until you could parse the insane humor
of the open world?

if asked I would tell you
to learn to see whole things & beings
be more frugal with trust than money
protect the innocent
work for the best for others
prepare for the worst from them
last: the yoruba say
all human beings
cover their nakedness
with other human beings
puzzle on that when you wonder

MUSCLE BEACH

i thank this dawn
for the timid sun so slow
to rise & bleach
the clouds above me
for the unmitigated arc
of the horizon

the waves that articulate
the infinite pacific
where float the mystic
nations west to east of here

the intimate cool
of the adamant air
as it tells the morning's
news to the inner edge
of my skin

for the sky-deep blue
of the ocean
whose rumors of long
fat fish tease
the pole-tending women
on the beach below
the ocean-deep
blue of the sky
& the gossiping sea birds
that swim in it

for the fading panel
of fog that lays
its scrim before
the mountains
at due north

the restless texture
of water
that carries my eye
out & out
to the state of imagination
past the end
of vision

the less than percussive
fizz of foam
when it settles on sand
for the pampered
toddler whose laughter
dares it
to catch her toes &
her first-time father
whose love rises
with the sun to rival
the depth
of sky & ocean

i thank this dawn
for casting me
small enough to recede
into the descending day
where i hover finite
not even a mote
imperceptible
before the light

THE WOMEN I HAVE NOT SLEPT WITH

For all my friends who have written tell-all memoirs

they number in the billions &
that's if i only count the living
for example, i have not slept with sarah palin &
not because she shoots large mammals for fun
i have not slept with her because
she's too far right & i'm too far left
& that's too much miscegenation to arouse
nor have i had sex with hillary clinton
though i did have a shot at hillary & i have a photograph to prove it
that's me shaking hands with her
head cocked to the side
a mating signal in every primate male
& i think i saw something in the curl of her mouth
but i couldn't make my move there in the gold room
with the line pushing at my back
but we'll see we'll see
i have not slept with madonna

before you get the impression
that i've only not slept with white women
i have not slept with oprah either
no fault of hers no fault of mine
we just never hooked up
never made it with vanessa williams & that one hurts
she once split from a sexual fantasy of mine
took one look at my admittedly adipose body & disappeared
from *my* fantasy
& wouldn't come back
broke my tumescent heart
& then there's chaka khan
sweet sweet sweet chaka

the lust of my life
i did get to hug her once
a nice belly to belly rub
but my boss was in the room
& it went nowhere
she sent me a box of chakalets

& so it goes or doesn't
if i haven't slept with you &
haven't mentioned you
please don't be offended
i thought you deserved your own poem

THE OLD FART'S LAMENT

i despair, i despair
i've lost my virtue & my hair
i'm sleeping in my underwear
but why tell you? you don't care

THE LAST OF MY TIME MAKES A CITY

the last of my time makes a city that fills
is filling now with all the music i have ever loved
sonatas for cellos & congas
choirs of saxophones / entire symphonies of scat & arias
in languages i've never learned but know the music of
this is where i live / this is how i feed
on memory & melody whose fey structures surround me
whose architects have shaped my time

but perhaps i make too much demand of song
could some other art better compose my summary years?
does the poem reach far enough / spread wide enough?
can i clear the stage of people whom i do not wish
to know? is my eye to be trusted after all
that it has seen? could my last city be well built on canvas
its thoroughfares curving & arcing in perspective
up past the smokestacks & bridges
where the factions of my years lob color bombs
at each other across the boulevard? no & no
my last time is a swinging tune in a minor key
in a town built of timbre with lithe ethnic dancers
& a hell of a band

2

i have come so very far & gone nowhere
memory wearied long ago & now rests with my youth
at the breach of paths old runaways like nat turner
wore across the Great Dismal Swamp where my home town floated
roots in memory / memory in roots
cottonmouth & cohorts of nocturnal forest felons hunted & mated there
(old nat you should have lived to die free in this slough

marooned with your brothers in its deadly safety)
so much leaf over the eye & under the foot
loam so alive each fallen twig bored down roots
vast orchestras of birds sang of me & other tourists of the swamp
the summer sun blinked down its checkerboard patterns
according to the whims of breeze & leaf
& i was at home with my serenity
until the perfidious dark chased me home

my city walk is no less shaded by time & euphony (the birds
sing a cappella here) no less the habitat of hunters & prey
i know where the ocean is / can smell it from here
can find the houses where the specters of my loves reside
can shop for melodies of every shade of humankind
some days my wealth enlarges me
for i own treasures as short as a four-beat phrase
or as long as that string of 16th notes
that trilled its way through my head just now
you i value most of all for the billowing love
that let you read this far
please describe for me the light we met inside of
did our breaths collide? i do not mind
that i can't recall the cubist planes of your face
but when you spoke how was your cadence tempered?
what was your favorite word?

3

in homer's time they tracked the body's hollows
for fumets of the soul
the colon seemed a likely host which we can understand
but i wonder: if they had captured one
what would they have done with it?
dyed it green & sealed it in a jar so natural philosophers
could worry it to death? nagged it for tutorials
in metaphysics until the poor thing bled ectoplasm?

i have read so much & learned so little
it's not just that age stutters the mind
that i can't recall the sequence of the presidents
or where the peloponnesus is
it's time's obliteration of all those smart ideas
that could have cued my life
knit together they might have told me
how we came to live in this kakistocracy & how to lead us out
how history defies hegel & adopts the progress
of the cottonmouth / mating in knots & shedding
its odious skin as it slithers along
it's that i can no longer sing on key
so what does it matter if i know a thousand
songs? it's that i can't chant the tribal story like a griot
or think my pea-green ass out of this goddamn jar

4

despite or because of all i remain a man of song
there's a boogie in my blood that palpitates
my body in the tempo of the present
in the presence of my children who are wiser & more comely
than i my low bass voice projects a dust of summer colors
as far as its range will carry
unlike me they have such perfect pitch
they do not have to sing to be understood
on the theme of karen i blow a mellow blues
of owing what i don't know how to pay
my vows swore me to clarify her dreams
pitch a brick into the eye of the cyclops that bars our way
& all i've done is compose a long confounding puzzle
even i have no solution for

so that's the quest i'm off on now
i'll drive till the map runs out
fly till i reverse the globe
spin & spin till i'm dervish enough to improvise a song
that's free of every image in this poem
transcribe that lyric
& you'll have my answer

A HOME BREW (RECAST)

there was a time when
we each needed a voice
but now?
your silences are more articulate
they sing between my ears
& the song has love in it
but not the kind that calls
me in the moment

it would be easier to describe
if we were speaking music
even in a silent song
there'd be a simultaneity
of voices / a function
for dissonance in the humming
of a minor chord perhaps e flat

but no / there is no harmony
when the voices are the same
only a strumming tension
that must resolve but how?

here is the instrument of me
still untuned as it vibrates in
the song of you / a strong wine
of a woman aging on my tongue

INTERLUDE

the sun is late behind the mountains
of puerto vallarta
sleepy waves stroke the sands
no gulls swoop & caw
the only voices of this morning
are the children's
as they splash & scream
at the foot of the bay

near the point where hill
slopes to cove
a lost gothic tower looks out
of the brilliant green
it is the house where john huston shot
Night of the Iguana in '64
karen sleeps / i write
there is no hint of that film's dry rot
in the room at this placid moment
i have not read the news for a week

i know this peace is contrived
& cannot be trusted
in the world beneath imagination
arsenals grow
nations snarl & snap
the right tugs away at time
the left tries to shove it forward

but for now it is enough to admire
the new sun's deletion of the milky way
the verdant depth of this green triangulation
light on the water
clouds under sun
the somnolent whisper of the waves

INTERLUDE 2

The Storm

at 4:15 the storm is punctual
& everything is change
the soft rain hardens
a thin august breeze
& now bends the perfect palms
thunder sounds
from the roof of the day
as lightning stabs the ficus
in the foothills over there

i find a contrary peace
in our earth's sudden violence
as i stand at the window with teddy wilson
on my ipad
              he is swinging precisely
with an ancient wisdom
only silent listeners learn
he is the antistorm

the squall exits west to cover
the dauntless ocean
as teddy wilson renews the day

in my years i have blown thunder
              i have spit lightning
              i have stood tranquil
              i have come & gone

INTERLUDE 3

Sunset

from the advancing shore i watch
the daily mounting of the myth
of the death of the sun

my prodigal storm has lost its eye
over the infinite water
a faint residue of the torrent
in a smear of grey at west-northwest
& dense black sky at west-southwest
is all that remains of the assault
upon the rainforest
at due west the clouds fragment &
an arm of wisp frames
the day's last sun whose storied
scarlet globe abates in descent
to magenta

horizon / orison
this sated day whelmed
in baptismal death
& renewal
a resolution unclogged
with summation
in consequence of light
fire into water
day into night

     slow fade to silver
     slow fade to black

SUMMER REQUIEM

out of the restless bowels
of a failed june day summer
has escaped its pink promise
& in its red breath foretells
the arrival of the constant beast
of uninvited change
wafting a burnt nourishment
through the black-floored corridors
of the city
                   upon our faces fall the showers
their first kisses sweet enough
but in the context of the bituminous
clouds whence they nested
they are the cherubim
of what booms & coruscates
the imminent torrents that will crash down
& rise up from the drains & drown our goods
                                        this tender breeze
is a threat of wind screaming wind's obscenities
through trembling bolted shutters
                        what lives
in fiery water & burning wind is elemental danger
its fell eyes reptilian
                   think of the mocs
& gators that swam into new orleans
that dismal summer not long ago when katrina blew
her frontline dirges & the white house
didn't care
               think of the macabre
bedtime anime that stalked you
from dream to childhood dream & all the adult genius
of humankind could not pour enough concrete
to cover it
               relax

we tell ourselves
                    it's only weather
the wars are distant
                    the taliban &
al qaeda are oceans deserts & mountains away
the nukes of pakistan & india & israel
are capped
                    the earthquakes in the waters
off honduras do not tremble our shelves
our walls are thick & guarded
the colors of our garden are in balance
nothing threatens us except the ambitions
of our fat cells & a dollar so weightless
it flies with the birds
                    answer:
the dna of the chthonic god of entropy
we made when we first learned to dream
he leads nothing knows nothing cares nothing
for sin or goodness
                    is nothing
but a falling apart & reconstitution
into some lesser thing
                    answer:
the coded colors of the hours
the daunting song we never learned
whose lyric was of stillness & flesh

put another way
the distance from fire to flood
is not time
the temperature
of human breath is not weather
the hours are in their heat
& will have us

A WINTER CONFESSION

in my many many years i never have been certain
of the things that i thought i knew
or trusted the honesty of what i have felt
or even the meaning of truth or feeling

if i were from an earlier age i would tie
these raveling ropes of reason & intuition
to this globe of snow floating outside my window
& winter's indelible image of death before renewal

outdoors among senescent branches depending
from frozen maples i find no gratitude that snow
chalks away this waste image of limbs become sticks
green leaves to the brown of funereal earth

hauling winter's pessimistic dreams across the yard
has me assigning baleful blame at the contradiction
of all this purity upon the barren streets
upon our screaming days seldom silent never true

i would wrap up this feeling of being lost at home
& take it to god if only god had the grace to be
instead i have no place to house my doubt
& not have it corrode the brightness of this day

in truth or not belief or not security or fear or not
we walk from here to there beside our best imitation
of naked time & its knocked-up protégé history
ugly & overdressed & clumsy in its moves

it would be a form of lie if i did not tell you that the base
of this reflection is that i can see from where i write
my actual death chuckling away in smug ambiguity
as if it were a great accomplishment to know

what all humankind has fought to know
from the last of now to the first of then
death is proud of our ignorance of time &
tells us it's a gift of peace passed off to us

as the root artifact of responsibility
but what crooked thing have we not done in our
ignorance? what have we the untold not bent down
what good thing have we not broken?

what ruin have we not sold as new?
we have all but killed the earth the sky
the waters & much of what has lived
within them as casually as a yawn

we the living have not earned a good green death

EVENING AGAIN

for Karen

i remind myself that it is only evening
& of course the sun has thinned its light
that darkness calls the city poem to be
the swollen generations who fill the day
close with the light & start their search
for love enough to still the rolling bassline
that swings a maudlin blues

note that in no known light
do named things rhyme today
that we must be contented with a tender assonance
with those we call in our true voices
as the evening song neither new nor better
hums & strums along

i write these lines because i want a record
of or for my spirit as it turns & starts for home
of the way it tuned itself to sing the evening song
a voice at ease among its strings & frets
secure in knowing that love enough awaits
to tell the difference between the silver chords
i know as home & the plainsong of the blues evaders

this is my current definition of love
you sing & are sung of
i hear & am heard

ON WAKING IN THE DARK

when
near the dawn of that bent night
i fell out of my last dream &
onto an unpaved road of antique youth
to black earth now rippled
by its muddy rain-fed lines
of sweet roasting-ear corn
elephant ear melons & fluffy
bushes with irish (or so we called them)
potatoes that swell beneath the roots
i asked my self why
it had brought me here
when my senses know only the acid
spoor of my crippled city?
why make memory oneiric matter
when it is so poorly
suited to the blurred vision
of an active sleep?

it is the need you do not know you have
i said to my self
the place the absent years
have cleared for you
sung with the sibilance
of new grown things so sharp
they mince the limber breeze

but these stanchions are of
the original deceit aren't they?
for when did dreams narrate
a clean sequential line
of images?
when did the conscious day
for that matter?

this gift of dream
from self to self
where innocence
rebuts the crimes you & the world
inflict upon each other by the hour
relieves but can't sustain
dreams must know you will dig
above them to perceive
the world as it is &
yourself as you are
unless they show to you
the obscure tracks of the self
but that's another poem

ACKNOWLEDGMENTS

This collection would not be without the tender care of the brilliant and accomplished Lauri Scheyer. Lauri knows my poetry better than I do. Many of my early poems were long-lost to me; poems that I had not seen in more than fifty years were at her fingertips and fresh in her mind. This alone made her participation invaluable.

Even more important was her informed and sensitive judgment of the newer work. We poets are jealous of our words; we take criticism poorly; we probably couldn't survive our own workshops. But it has always been easy to trust Lauri's opinions. Ever since I returned to the medium in the mid-1990s I have sent new pieces to her for comment, which she has given honestly and with x-ray insight. She has been reading over my shoulder as I have written for several decades now, and I have always reached for her standard.

During the years that we have been assembling this collection I have relied upon her scholar's experience in sequence, selection, and revision. The poems that grew out of me in this term have been read by Lauri in every draft, and there have been many drafts. Not once have I heard her scream through my computer when I found a better word for a new poem or a poem that was fifty years old.

So thank you, Dr. Scheyer, for your patience, and insight. No poet has ever had a better muse.

*

Lauri Scheyer wishes to thank A. B. Spellman for his trust and for sharing so openly and intimately the literary processes of a brilliant poet. It has been the gift and learning experience of a lifetime to closely observe his creative path and offer any humble assistance. He has my constant respect and affection for his poetry and for the way his humanity infuses his writing and ways of being in the world. Thank you, A. B. Never anything but a joy and an honor.

*

A. B. Spellman and Lauri Scheyer wish to thank the previous publishers of some of these poems, many of which appeared then in different versions. We also thank Wesleyan University Press for their extraordinary support and enthusiasm at each step of this book's preparation. Above all, our heartfelt gratitude goes to Suzanna Tamminen, to the anonymous readers of the prospectus, and to the editorial board. And we are deeply indebted to designer Mindy Basinger Hill, production coordinator Jim Schley, copyeditor Ally Findley, marketing manager Jaclyn Wilson, and publicist Stephanie Elliott Prieto.

page 4   "Nocturne for Eric" was originally published in *The Floating Bear* 12 (1961).

page 46   "When Black People Are" first appeared in *Journal of Black Poetry* 1, no. 10 (Fall 1968).

page 85   "A Home Brew (1960)" (dated 11/1960) appeared in *The Floating Bear* 25 (1961).

page 86   "A Theft of Wishes" appeared in *Beyond the Blues*, ed. Rosey E. Pool (Lympne , Kent, UK: Hand and Flower Press, 1962).

page 88   "There Is in the Atlanta" appeared in *The Journal of Black Poetry* 1, no. 10 (Fall 1968).

page 90   "Did John's Music Kill Him?" first appeared in *The Militant Black Writer in Africa and the United States*, eds. Mercer Cook and Stephen E. Henderson (New York: Morrow, 1969).

page 91   "The Beautiful Day X (2020)" was first written in 1966, then revised in 2020.

pages 139 and 141   "Jeff's Poems 3" and "Jeff's Poems 4" are from a set that was commissioned by the composer Jeff Scott in honor of his stepfather. They are composed for ease of oral delivery.

page 155   "A Home Brew (recast)" was reworked in 2020 from the 1960 poem of the same name. A. B. Spellman revises his poems extensively and continuously, often looking back to see how he can extend themes explored in earlier poems as he constantly reworks his evolving vision. For this reason, it is important to him in some cases for earlier and revised versions to co-exist, as with "A Homebrew." In such instances, two versions of these poems have been included in this volume.

ABOUT THE AUTHOR AND EDITOR

ALFRED BENNETT (A. B.) SPELLMAN JR. was born on August 7, 1935, in Elizabeth City, North Carolina. Both of his parents were educators. He earned his high school diploma from P. W. Moore High School, where he was a member of the basketball team, glee club, and oratorical club. In 1956, Spellman earned his BS degree in political science from Howard University. While at Howard, he was active in the chorus and the Howard Players, and he began his writing career. After graduating, Spellman enrolled in the Howard University Law School. By 1959, Spellman was working as a writer, reviewing jazz artists and music for magazines such as *Metronome* and *Downbeat*, and in 1964 he published his first book of poems, *The Beautiful Days*. In 1966, he published his first nonfiction book, *Four Lives in the Bebop Business*, an in-depth look at the lives of musicians Cecil Taylor, Ornette Coleman, Herbie Nichols, and Jackie McLean. The following year, Spellman joined a group of black poets touring the nation's historically black colleges. From 1968 until 1969, he worked as a political essayist and poet for *Rhythm* magazine, and in 1969 he conducted a lecture series throughout the country, teaching at various colleges including Morehouse, Emory, and Rutgers. In 1972, Spellman was hired to teach African American studies at Harvard University, where he remained until 1975, when he became director of the Arts in Education Study Project for the National Endowment of the Arts (NEA) in Washington, DC. Spellman worked at the NEA for three decades, until his retirement in 2005, serving as director of the Arts Endowment Expansion Program, special assistant to the chair, acting deputy chair for programs, associate deputy for program coordination, director of the Office of Guidelines and Panel Operations, then deputy chair for the Office of Guidelines, Panel, and Council Operations. In his retirement Spellman has continued to serve as an advocate for the arts, including as an advisor for the Rockefeller Panel on Arts, Education and Americans, the Jazz Advisory Group, and the Smithsonian Institution's National Museum of African American History & Culture.

LAURI SCHEYER earned a PhD in English and American literature at the University of Chicago with a specialization in poetry and poetics. She is Xiaoxiang Distinguished Professor at Hunan Normal University (China), where she directs the British and American Poetry Research Center. Her books include *A History of African American Poetry, Slave Songs and the Birth of African American Poetry, The Heritage Series of Black Poetry, 1962–1975, Theatres of War,* and *Selected Poems of Calvin C. Hernton,* co-edited with David Grundy (also published by Wesleyan University Press).